Park Avenue Potluck
CELEBRATIONS

The Society of Memorial Sloan-Kettering Cancer Center

Park Avenue Potluck

CELEBRATIONS

ENTERTAINING AT HOME WITH

New York's Savviest Hostesses

FLORENCE FABRICANT

PHOTOGRAPHS BY BEN FINK

RIZZOLI
NEW YORK

THE SOCIETY OF MEMORIAL SLOAN-KETTERING CANCER CENTER
GIVES OUR HEARTFELT THANKS TO THE FOLLOWING COMPANIES WHO
HAVE GENEROUSLY SUPPORTED *Park Avenue Potluck Celebrations.*

CREATIVE CAKES, INC.
GREYLEDGE FARM ALL-NATURAL BLACK ANGUS BEEF
LOBEL'S OF NEW YORK
MRS. MONOGRAM

First published in the United States of America in 2009 by
Rizzoli International Publications, Inc.
300 Park Avenue South
New York, NY 10010
www.rizzoliusa.com

2009 2010 2011 2012 / 10 9 8 7 6 5 4 3 2 1

Distributed in the U.S. trade by Random House, New York

Designed by Patricia Fabricant
Food styling by Susan Sugarman
Back endpaper photo by Laurie Lambrecht

Printed in Singapore

ISBN-13: 978-0-8478-3344-3

Library of Congress Control Number: 2009925847

Dedicated to the patients of
Memorial Sloan–Kettering Cancer Center,
as well as their families and caregivers.

The Society of Memorial Sloan–Kettering Cancer Center

COOKBOOK COMMITTEE

Kathy Thomas—*Co-Chairman*
Barbara Tollis—*Co-Chairman*
Heather Leeds—*Vice Chairman*
Wendy Arriz
Muffie Potter Aston
Chesie Breen
Catherine Carey
Nancy Mulholland Conroy
Chiara Edmands
Kelly Forsberg
Elizabeth Fuller

Eugenie Niven Goodman
Leslie Heaney
Coco Kopelman
Nicole Limbocker
Stephanie Loeffler
Barbara McLaughlin
Leslie Perkin
Sarah S. Powers
George Rudenauer
Tracy Snyder
Alexandra Wernink

We would like to give our sincerest gratitude to Maryanne Greenfield, Executive Director of The Society; Jacqueline Blandi, Associate Director; Megan Mitchell, Individual Giving & Special Projects Manager; and Assistants China Gordon, Caroline Nguyen, and Lauren Robinson for the individual talent and passion that they contributed to the book. Together, The Society's staff is magical.

RECIPE AND ENTERTAINING CONTRIBUTORS

Wendy Arriz
Muffie Potter Aston
Patrice Bell
Kathy Binder
Felicia Blum
Chesie and Tommy Breen
Tory Burch
Susan Burke
Virginia Burke
Catherine Carey
Shelley and Michael Carr
Nancy Coffey

Katie Colgate
Alicia Bouzán Cordon
Dianne G. Crary
Jennifer Creel
Mary Darling
Mary Davidson
Caroline and Tom Dean
Virginia Dean
Amy Raiter Dwek
Ingrid Edelman
Webb Egerton
Florence Fabricant

Food and Nutrition, Memorial
Sloan-Kettering Cancer Center
Kelly Forsberg
Martha Kramer Fox
Elizabeth Fuller
Sallie and Mark Giordano
Eugenie Niven Goodman
Anne Grauso
Maryanne Greenfield
Jamee Gregory
Samantha Gregory
Stephanie Griswold
Shoshanna and Josh Gruss
Alexia Hamm Ryan and Baird Ryan
Barbara Harbach
Laura Harris
Tammy Harris
Janine Haspel
Leslie and Andrew Heaney
Fernanda and Kirk Henckels
Alison Barr Howard
Kelley Johnston
Leslie and Peter D. Jones
Robyn and Kenneth Joseph
Kathleen King
Shirley Maytag King
Coco and Arie L. Kopelman
Anki and Doug Leeds
Heather Leeds
Natalie Leeds Leventhal
Nicole and Derek Limbocker
Stephanie Loeffler
Helena Martinez
Mary McCabe, R.N., M.A.

Lisa and Brian McCarthy
Barbara and Kevin McLaughlin
Lori Meyerson
Mary Mitchell
Megan Mitchell
Melissa and Chappy Morris
Martha O'Brien
Claudia Overstrom
Deborah Panaiotopoulos
Caroline Perkin
Leslie Perkin
Nina Pickett
Ashley Potter
Sarah S. Powers
Charlotte Reardon
Annette U. Rickel, Ph.D.
Donna Rosen
George Rudenauer
Bobbie Jean Sabbatini
Burwell and Chip Schorr
Betty and Virgil Sherrill
Kitty and Stephen Sherrill
Tracy and Jay Snyder
Daisy Soros
Laurie Sykes
Kathy Thomas
Kimberly Tighe
Barbara Tollis
Yolanda Toth
Maria Villalba
Patsy Warner
Alexandra Wernink
Judith Winslow

Contents

A Note from the Chairman of Memorial Sloan-Kettering Cancer Center

~※~

We are grateful to The Society of Memorial Sloan-Kettering, Florence Fabricant, and Rizzoli Publications for producing a book that celebrates family and friends with everything from good home-cooked meals to abundant special occasion feasts. *Park Avenue Potluck Celebrations* is filled with recipes that have endured the test of time and embodies The Society's legacy of caring and giving. A portion of the proceeds from the *Park Avenue Potluck* series helps to support the Society's many programs in patient care, research, education, and treatment of cancer.

For more than six decades, The Society of MSKCC has served as an inspiration—for us, within the Memorial Sloan-Kettering community, as well as for other organizations that rely on voluntary service to make a difference in the lives of others. To the members of The Society, we are indebted to you for your tireless dedication to helping patients, raising funds to support critical needs at MSKCC, and improving public understanding of cancer.

DOUGLAS A. WARNER III
CHAIRMAN
BOARDS OF OVERSEERS AND MANAGERS

Preface

On behalf of The Society of Memorial Sloan-Kettering Cancer Center, I want to extend our heartfelt thank you to the readers who supported our first cookbook, *Park Avenue Potluck*, and to those of you who have now purchased our second book, *Park Avenue Potluck Celebrations.* Partial proceeds from the sale of both books help us to support vital programs dedicated to promoting the well-being of patients, supporting cancer research, and providing public education on the prevention, early detection, and treatment of cancer.

Of the many tributes *Park Avenue Potluck* has received, what has probably been most gratifying to us has been hearing from many patients who regard the book as a celebration of survivorship. So we could not think of a more appropriate theme for our follow-up than Celebrations — a toast to wellness and survivorship, as well as a peek into the homes and lives of New Yorkers dedicated to serving patients and families through volunteer service. The book has been a labor of love by members of The Society — and others — who have contributed special occasion recipes and entertaining style tips that we hope will warm your hearts and grace your tables as they do ours.

In 1946, The Society of MSKCC was founded by a small group of women who wanted to do whatever they could to make the MSKCC patient experience more comfortable. This legacy of compassion has been handed down from one generation of Society members to the next, in the belief that volunteerism is a fundamental public virtue that makes our nation great.

We are all committed to Memorial Sloan-Kettering's mission — to provide the best cancer care available anywhere. We are grateful to Florence Fabricant and Rizzoli Publications for their continued partnership in putting together this collection of celebration recipes. It reflects our hearts and souls. The same warmth and care that we devote to MSKCC's patients and their families, we have used to prepare the family celebrations that we share with you in these pages.

LESLIE M. JONES
PRESIDENT
THE SOCIETY OF MEMORIAL SLOAN-KETTERING CANCER CENTER,
2007–2009

Foreword

   ⚮

Two years ago, the members of The Society of Memorial Sloan–
Kettering Cancer Center generously opened their recipe files, searched
their memories, and sought cooking tips from friends and family to make
Park Avenue Potluck a reality. Now they have done it again. This time they
contributed scores of new recipes that are especially suited to the many, and
different, occasions that fill their calendars.

  For each of the celebrations outlined in this new look at *Potluck,* they have
also revealed the techniques and even some "trade secrets" that experienced
hostesses rely on to give real personality to the various celebratory dinners,
lunches, brunches, and parties they throw. It's these touches, many achieved
with help from the treasured sources listed in the back of the book, that
set the events apart and make them memorable and enjoyable for all the
participants, including the party-givers.

  The hostesses satisfy their guests with good food and drink, often in
settings that dazzle with themed creativity, and always in an atmosphere of
welcoming generosity and consideration. They now share this know-how.

  Perhaps there will be clever invitations that add to the anticipation
leading up to an occasion. A note in a bottle for a beach picnic, or a photo
of the guests of honor for an anniversary are typical of these ladies' flair.
Will it be a costume party for Halloween? Then, guests who shy from coming
in fancy dress will be offered upon their arrival a basket of hats and masks
assembled by the hostess. A children's birthday party will have properly
Lilliputian chairs and tables for the youngsters. Every chapter in this book is
filled with suggestions like these to add to the pleasure of a gathering.

The menus have been designed for seamless facility, with recipes that usually accommodate advance preparation. Keeping an eye on the calendar, as one must for celebrations that come along during the year, pertains to the menus and recipes. Thanks to the plethora of good ideas from the members I was able to select bright salads and seasonal vegetables for summer enticements—just as apples, nuts, and glowing pumpkins enrich events in fall. Alternate recipes scattered throughout the book are suggested for each of the menus.

The contributors have also shared memories and family traditions that sweeten these occasions and give deeper meaning to the various dishes served at these happy times. I feel honored that I was able to cook my way through a second *Potluck,* to assemble and to write it, knowing that the Memorial Sloan-Kettering Cancer Center would benefit from the result.

FLORENCE FABRICANT

An Intimate Evening
VALENTINE'S DAY

Valentine's Day offers an occasion for a quiet little
celebration—a twosome or a few couples sharing a
relaxed but elegant dinner, preferably at home.
The menu can center around a luxurious indulgence
or simpler, but favorite fare. Romance, or the notion
of it, will be in the air, so plan on lovely flowers for the
table, candles (always unscented so they don't interfere
with the aromas of food and wine), and even soft music
that might inspire a close dance. And don't forget
chocolate truffles with the dessert.

"My Cardinal Rule of Entertaining: Relax
and enjoy yourself. When you're at ease and
having a great time, your guests will too—I
guarantee it! Nothing stifles a party faster
than a stiff hostess."

—Muffie Potter Aston

"I like to have a very casual easygoing feel
at dinner. However, I do think seating is
very important and therefore I also use place
cards. For Valentine's Day I put heart-
shaped sugar cookies with names written in
icing at each place. For family dinners I have
had my children make the place cards."

—Alexandra Wernink

~ THE MENU ~

CHARLENE'S ARTICHOKE SOUP WITH OYSTERS

FILET MIGNON À LA CRÈME

BEVERLY'S MALTESE POTATOES

WARM PEPPER-DRESSED MANGO

BESSO'S FEATHERY PECAN PUFFS

CHOCOLATE TRUFFLES (FROM YOUR FAVORITE SHOP)

Because the menu is meant for two—though it can be expanded to serve four—it involves more complex preparation than many of the celebrations that are on a grander scale. Each dish calls for some last-minute kitchen work, which can be done by one with the other looking on. And as a result, it is a dinner that proceeds at a leisurely pace, with some time elapsed between courses.

A very dry Champagne or a white wine like muscadet or sauvignon blanc should accompany the first course, followed by a red wine, as luxurious a bottle as you can afford, like a good Bordeaux or a California cabernet sauvignon, for the main course. A sweet wine, a Sauternes, or an ice wine, for example, would complement the dessert.

ALSO SUGGESTED: *Pomegranate Mimosas (page 77), Smooth Broccoli Soup (page 214), Penne alla Vodka with Scallops (page 50), Derek's Shrimp with Tomato Sauce (page 92), Perfect Parisian Salad (page 97), Prosciutto and Arugula Salad (page 55), Roaring Twenties Coffee Bavarian Cream (page 206), Flourless Dark Chocolate Cake (page 42)*

Charlene's Artichoke Soup with Oysters

My mother received this recipe from a friend about thirty years ago. She serves it in Champagne glasses at dinner parties, followed by beef tenderloin.

Makes 2 servings

1 (9-ounce) package frozen artichokes, thawed
1½ cups chicken stock
1 tablespoon lemon juice
1 tablespoon unsalted butter
1 tablespoon all-purpose flour
2 tablespoons heavy cream
Salt and freshly ground black pepper
6 oysters, with their liquor

Place the artichokes and stock in a medium saucepan over medium-high heat and bring to a simmer. Reduce the heat and simmer just until heated through. Add the lemon juice, transfer to a blender, and puree. Force through a sieve to remove any solid bits.

Melt the butter in a saucepan, whisk in the flour, and stir in the pureed soup. Bring to a simmer and cook until slightly thickened. Stir in the cream and season with salt and pepper.

Just before serving, divide the oysters between 2 soup plates. Add the liquor to the soup and bring to a simmer. At the table, spoon the soup over and around the oysters.

If you shuck your own oysters, be sure to do it over a bowl to catch the juices, or liquor, which you must then strain before using. If you buy the oysters shucked, be sure to ask for the liquor.

Filet Mignon à la Crème

I SURPRISED LESLIE, WHO IS NOW MY WIFE, ON VALENTINE'S DAY WITH A FABULOUS DINNER AT HOME—AND A PROPOSAL OF MARRIAGE! THIS RECIPE HAS BEEN OUR FAVORITE EVER SINCE THAT MEMORABLE MEAL. WE LOVE TO MAKE IT TOGETHER FOR OUR FAMILY AND FRIENDS FOR ANY CELEBRATION.

MAKES 2 SERVINGS

1 TABLESPOON UNSALTED BUTTER
2 FILET MIGNONS, EACH ABOUT 1½ INCHES THICK
1 MEDIUM SHALLOT, FINELY CHOPPED
5 WHITE MUSHROOMS, THINLY SLICED
2 TABLESPOONS COGNAC
½ CUP HEAVY CREAM
1 TEASPOON DIJON MUSTARD
SALT AND FRESHLY GROUND BLACK PEPPER

Melt the butter in a heavy skillet, preferably cast-iron, over medium-high heat. When hot, add the steaks and sear for about 3 minutes on each side, a trifle less than medium rare. Remove them to a plate and tent with foil to keep warm.

Add the shallot and mushrooms to the skillet, reduce the heat, and sauté until the mushrooms have wilted, about 5 minutes. Add the Cognac and stir. Add the cream, stirring constantly, until the mixture achieves a saucelike consistency. Stir in the mustard and season with salt and pepper to taste.

Return the steaks and any accumulated juices to the skillet. Reheat over low heat and baste the steaks. Serve immediately.

The filet steaks will probably be tied with butcher's cord.
Be sure to snip and discard it before serving.

DEBORAH PANAIOTOPOULOS

Beverly's Maltese Potatoes

I WAS FORTUNATE ENOUGH TO ACCOMPANY MY SISTER, PAMELA, ON ONE OF HER TRIPS TO VILLA BELVEDERE ON MALTA TO VISIT HER MOTHER-IN-LAW, BEVERLY FRENCO-RANDON. BEVERLY WAS A MASTERFUL COOK WHO ENTERTAINED REGULARLY AT THE FAMILY SEASIDE VILLA. THIS POTATO DISH HAS BECOME A FAVORITE ON BOTH SIDES OF THE ATLANTIC, IN PART FOR THE INVITING SCENT IT DELIVERS AS IT BAKES.

MAKES 2 SERVINGS

12 SMALL RED POTATOES, SCRUBBED
1 MEDIUM ONION, QUARTERED
2 CLOVES GARLIC, SLICED
3 TABLESPOONS EXTRA VIRGIN OLIVE OIL
Salt AND FRESHLY GROUND BLACK PEPPER
2 SPRIGS FRESH ROSEMARY
2 SPRIGS FRESH THYME

Preheat the oven to 375 degrees.

Place the potatoes in a small baking dish. Add the onion and garlic. Drizzle with the oil, dust generously with salt and pepper, and toss the ingredients together. Scatter the leaves from the rosemary and thyme over the dish.

Place in the oven and bake for about 40 minutes, turning the ingredients from time to time. Increase the oven temperature to 450 degrees and bake for a few more minutes, until crispy, and serve immediately.

If you prefer, the potatoes can be peeled. And in warm weather, increase the quantities for an excellent roasted potato salad to include in a buffet.

"The year starts out slowly, with little entertaining until Valentine's Day, when a quiet supper, preferably at home in front of the fireplace, is a tradition."
—Leslie Perkin

"Wherever we live we always have a piano so I try to remember to have it tuned. We are a musical family, and whatever the occasion, guests seem to love to sing after dinner."
—Susan Burke

AMY RAITER DWEK

Warm Pepper-Dressed Mango

〜〜

AFTER COLLEGE, MY FIRST JOB WAS WORKING FOR *Bon Appétit* MAGAZINE. THIS WAS A RECIPE THOUGHT TO BE VERY "GOURMET" THAT I DREAMED UP AND MADE AT THAT TIME, WITH GREAT SUCCESS, FOR A SMALL DINNER PARTY. I HAVE BEEN MAKING IT EVER SINCE, FOR AS FEW AS TWO PEOPLE AND AS MANY AS TWELVE.

MAKES 2 SERVINGS

1 RIPE MANGO
1 TABLESPOON UNSALTED BUTTER
COARSELY GROUND BLACK PEPPER
1 TABLESPOON SUGAR
VANILLA ICE CREAM OR FROZEN YOGURT FOR SERVING

Slice the mango in half vertically; peel and pit it. Slice the halves lengthwise into eighths. Chop any mango from around the pit.

Melt the butter in a small skillet over medium heat. Add the mango strips and pieces, dust with pepper and the sugar, and sauté a few minutes until lightly browned. Divide among 2 plates, spooning the pan juices over the fruit, and serve with ice cream or frozen yogurt.

❦ There is a new gadget on the market designed for removing the pit of a ❦ mango that is very effective. If you are a mango-lover, it is worth owning.

"My grandmother in San Diego would throw a Valentine's Day party for her grandchildren. All the Valentine cards would be in a big box covered in shiny red foil and decorated with heart-shaped doilies. We would then have her special sugar cookies and tea."
—Kelly Forsberg

Besso's Feathery Pecan Puffs

MY GRANDMOTHER WAS A GREAT BAKER, AND THESE FEATHER-
LIGHT TREATS THAT MELT IN YOUR MOUTH WERE ALWAYS ON
THE TABLE FOR SPECIAL OCCASIONS.

MAKES ABOUT 20

2 LARGE EGG WHITES
2 CUPS SUGAR
1 TEASPOON WHITE VINEGAR
1 TEASPOON VANILLA EXTRACT
PINCH OF SALT
2 CUPS CHOPPED PECANS

Preheat the oven to 300 degrees and line a baking sheet with parchment paper.

Place the egg whites in an electric mixer. Beat until just starting to form peaks, then gradually add the sugar, beating constantly. Beat in the vinegar, vanilla, and salt. Fold in the pecans.

Drop the mixture by mounds onto the baking sheet about 2 inches apart, place in the oven, and bake for about 15 minutes, until fairly firm. Cool before serving.

Store pecans and other nuts in the freezer to keep them fresh.

"There must be lots of candles, a fire in the fireplace, and Champagne. Valentine's Day is better at home than in restaurants."

—Leslie Jones

A Symbolic Dinner
PASSOVER

Passover is an eight-day holiday. The first and second nights are celebrated at the table with a service read before dinner from a prayer book called a Haggadah that essentially recounts and interprets the story of the Book of Exodus in the Bible. Many symbolic foods are either presented or eaten during the service at the start of this Seder dinner.

A dense mixture of chopped fruits and nuts called haroseth represents the mortar the Jews who were prisoners in Egypt used to construct the pyramids. Bitter herbs stand for life's travails. A sweet herb, like parsley, represents spring, but is dipped in salt water to represent the tears of suffering. A roasted shank bone is the symbol of ancient ritual sacrifice and eggs stand for rebirth. The dinner is often accompanied by festive songs.

～ THE MENU ～

Silken Mushroom Soup
Short Ribs Bourguignon
Ali's Mixed Holiday Salad
Flourless Dark Chocolate Cake
Fresh strawberries

"My friend Kathy has introduced many family traditions to her Seder. Everyone around the table is asked to say what it means to be free in today's world, to bring the story of Passover into the present day. At one point in the service, the leader squeezes the hand of the person next to him or her, and that person squeezes the hand of the next person, and so on. This sends the blessing around the table and makes everyone feel closer."
—Maryanne Greenfield

There are Jews in every part of the world, and the traditional dishes they might serve for the Passover dinner reflect their heritage. But all have in common the prohibition against any kind of leavening or flour during the eight-day holiday period. In New York, the Seder dinner menu for the first and second nights often has its roots in Eastern Europe. Chicken soup with matzo balls, chopped fish dumplings called gefilte fish served with horseradish, roast chicken or braised beef brisket, fruit and vegetable casseroles, and coconut macaroons are typical. This menu is a variation, starting with a mushroom soup, followed by braised short ribs (also called flanken), a salad, and an intense flourless chocolate cake.

Excellent kosher red or white wines are now being made in a dozen countries, so the choices for the Seder table are many. But one goblet should be filled and placed in the center of the table as "Elijah's cup" and reserved for any unexpected guests, who must be welcomed to the dinner. It is also traditional to leave the front door ajar, as a sign of welcome, something that is pretty easy to do in a New York apartment!

ALSO SUGGESTED: *Chilled Minted Zucchini Soup (page 90), Smooth Broccoli Soup (page 214), Perfect Parisian Salad (page 97), Sweet and Sour Red Cabbage (page 167), Beverly's Maltese Potatoes (page 25), Kathleen's Wheat-Free Fudge Brownies (page 130), Besso's Feathery Pecan Puffs (page 30)*

Silken Mushroom Soup

THIS RECIPE GOES BACK MORE THAN FORTY YEARS. IT WAS GIVEN TO MY MOTHER BY A FRIEND WHEN WE WERE LIVING IN OXFORD, ENGLAND, AND HAD NO CENTRAL HEATING. MY MOTHER OFTEN SERVES IT AS A STARTER FOR A HOLIDAY MEAL, AND IT HAS BECOME A FAMILY FAVORITE.

MAKES 6 TO 8 SERVINGS

3 TABLESPOONS EXTRA VIRGIN OLIVE OIL
1½ CUPS FINELY CHOPPED ONIONS
1 POUND WHITE MUSHROOMS, TRIMMED AND SLICED
6 CUPS WELL-FLAVORED CHICKEN STOCK
2 BAY LEAVES
SALT AND FRESHLY GROUND BLACK PEPPER

Heat the oil in a 4-quart saucepan over low heat. Add the onions and cook until they are softened but not browned, about 5 minutes. Add the mushrooms, cook for 5 minutes, or until softened, then add the chicken stock and bay leaves. Raise the heat to medium, bring to a simmer, and simmer for 20 minutes. Season with salt and pepper to taste and remove the bay leaves.

Puree the soup in a food processor or blender in several batches. Return the soup to the saucepan and reheat just before serving.

Chicken soup may be one of the staple dishes of a Seder, but this mushroom soup, with its base of good chicken stock (use homemade if possible), is a welcome variation, especially for those who would rather not tackle making matzo balls! And if you do plan to make your own chicken stock, a great trick is to simmer your whole chicken and vegetables in chicken broth, packaged or homemade, instead of in water, for a "double" stock that will be doubly flavorful.

If you are adept at making matzo balls, they can be served in this soup, especially if you add some finely minced sautéed mushrooms to the matzo batter.

Short Ribs Bourguignon

GERTIE SCHILLING, A WONDERFUL SWISS WOMAN, WAS MY GRANDPARENTS' COOK. SHE WAS WITH US UNTIL SHE DIED AT NINETY-NINE. GERTIE TAUGHT ME HOW TO ROAST A THANKSGIVING TURKEY WITH ALL THE TRIMMINGS AND TO MAKE A FABULOUS BEEF BOURGUIGNON, WHICH I HAVE RELIED ON FOR MANY CELEBRATIONS FOR MY FRIENDS AND FAMILY. THE AROMAS THAT WAFT THROUGH THE HOUSE ALWAYS BRING BACK MEMORIES OF HAPPY TIMES, ESPECIALLY WHEN GERTIE WAS COOKING FOR OUR FAMILY. IT IS VERY EASY TO MAKE FOR EITHER A SMALL DINNER PARTY OR A LARGER GATHERING.

MAKES 8 TO 10 SERVINGS

½ CUP POTATO STARCH

SEA SALT AND FRESHLY GROUND BLACK PEPPER

1 TEASPOON HERBES DE PROVENCE

5 POUNDS BEEF SHORT RIBS, CUT INTO 2-INCH CHUNKS, WITH BONE

1 TABLESPOON EXTRA VIRGIN OLIVE OIL OR GRAPESEED OIL

6 CLOVES GARLIC, SLICED

1 CUP BEEF STOCK

1 LARGE SWEET ONION, CHOPPED

1½ CUPS DRY RED WINE

3 SPRIGS FRESH THYME

16 SMALL WHITE ONIONS, ABOUT 1 INCH IN DIAMETER

16 BABY RED POTATOES

6 CARROTS, PEELED AND CUT ON THE DIAGONAL INTO 1-INCH CHUNKS

❧ Short ribs, a meltingly rich cut of beef, are the same as flanken, so adored on ❧ the Jewish–American table. In this recipe they are treated like beef bourguignon. Just be sure to use one of the excellent kosher red wines that are available when preparing them for a Seder. If the stew is made in advance, you can remove the bones after it has cooled for a more elegant presentation.

Mix the potato starch with salt and pepper to taste and the herbes de Provence and dust the meat with this mixture.

Heat the oil in a large (6- to 8-quart) casserole or Dutch oven. Add the garlic and cook briefly until softened but not browned. Remove the garlic and reserve it. Add the beef, a few pieces at a time, and brown them, removing them to a bowl as they are seared. Do not crowd them in the pan.

When the meat has been browned and removed, whisk the stock into the pot. Add the sweet onion and the reserved garlic. Stir in the wine and bring it to a simmer. Return the meat to the casserole, baste it, and add the thyme. Cover and simmer for 1 hour.

Meanwhile, bring a large pot of salted water to a boil, add the small white onions, and blanch them for 3 minutes. Use a slotted spoon to scoop them out. Cool, then peel them. Add the potatoes to the boiling water and cook for 10 minutes, or until tender. Drain. Once the meat has cooked for 1 hour, check the seasonings and add the potatoes and carrots. After another 30 minutes, add the small onions and cook until the meat is tender, another 15 to 30 minutes. Skim off any excess fat, remove from the heat, and check the seasonings again. Reheat the meat and vegetables shortly before serving.

"When we are not celebrating Passover with my husband's family, we have Passover Seder at the home of either my cousins Lori and Doug or my dear friend Kathy. As with all Seder dinners, their tables are set with the finest china and silverware to celebrate the importance of this meal. I am always so grateful to them for preserving and celebrating the traditions of this holy day and festival, especially for all of the children. Lori has a beautiful Seder plate that she fills with all the foods that symbolize Passover and this joyful time of year. She always hides the matzo, the Passover 'dessert,' and the children love searching for it no matter how young or old they are. Then all the guests gather together to sing Passover songs."

—Maryanne Greenfield

Ali's Mixed Holiday Salad

I FIRST CAME UP WITH THIS SALAD AS I WAS RUMMAGING THROUGH THE REFRIGERATOR FOR INGREDIENTS. YOU CAN VARY IT IN ANY WAY YOU WISH. SOMETIMES I ADD LONG, THIN CARROT SLICES, THINLY SLICED RADISHES, AND FRESH DILL. AND IF YOU SERVE THE DRESSING ON THE SIDE, ANY LEFTOVER SALAD WILL KEEP FOR A FEW DAYS.

MAKES 8 TO 10 SERVINGS

2 CUPS DRIED CHERRIES OR CRANBERRIES
2 CUCUMBERS, PEELED, CUT IN HALF, SEEDED, AND THINLY SLICED
¾ CUP CHOPPED TOASTED WALNUTS
2 TABLESPOONS GRATED ORANGE ZEST
¼ CUP WHITE WINE VINEGAR
¼ CUP EXTRA VIRGIN OLIVE OIL
¼ CUP WALNUT OIL
4 TART APPLES, PEELED, CORED, AND DICED
1 LARGE BOX OR BAG MIXED LETTUCE LEAVES
1 BUNCH ARUGULA, STEMS REMOVED

Place the cherries or cranberries in a small bowl, pour boiling water over them, and set aside to soak for 30 minutes. Drain and dry them on paper towels. Place them in a salad bowl with the cucumbers, walnuts, and orange zest. Whisk in the vinegar and the oils. Add the apples and set aside.

Shortly before serving, add the lettuce leaves and arugula, toss, and serve.

Using nut oil in combination with olive oil adds an intriguing touch to a dressing, especially if there are nuts in the salad. Try to match the type of oil to the kind of nuts you are using.

Flourless Dark Chocolate Cake

THIS RECIPE WAS GIVEN TO ME MANY MOONS AGO WHEN I VISITED SOME DEAR SPANISH FRIENDS IN BUENOS AIRES. IT'S FOR THE TRUE CHOCOHOLIC—VERY, VERY RICH.

MAKES AT LEAST 10 SUPERRICH SERVINGS

2 STICKS (½ POUND) UNSALTED BUTTER

1 CUP RAISINS OR DRIED CURRANTS

½ CUP BRANDY OR WHISKEY, WARMED

½ POUND GOOD-QUALITY BITTERSWEET CHOCOLATE
(ABOUT 70 PERCENT CACAO), CUT INTO PIECES

6 LARGE EGGS

1½ CUPS SUPERFINE SUGAR

1 TABLESPOON POTATO STARCH

1 TEASPOON VANILLA EXTRACT

UNSWEETENED WHIPPED CREAM FOR SERVING, OPTIONAL

Preheat the oven to 325 degrees. Use a little of the butter to grease a 10-inch cake pan.

Place the raisins or currants in a bowl, add the warm brandy or whiskey, and set aside. Place the remaining butter and the chocolate in a saucepan and melt them over low heat. Stir. (The butter and chocolate can also be melted in a microwave oven for about 1 minute.)

In a large bowl, beat the eggs and sugar until well blended, pale, and creamy, about 4 minutes. Sift the potato starch and fold it in. Stir in the chocolate and butter mixture, then stir in the raisins or currants and brandy and the vanilla.

Pour the batter into the pan and bake for about 40 minutes, until the cake has firmed up on top but a tester does not come out perfectly clean. It should be slightly underdone. Remove from the oven and cool to room temperature, then cover and refrigerate for at least 3 hours or overnight.

Remove the cake from the refrigerator and unmold it 1 hour before serving.

❧ If kosher observance prevents you from serving a butter-based cake at ❧
the end of a meal, a good-quality margarine (not the soft-spread kind) can be
substituted for the butter in the cake. When not making this cake for Passover,
2 tablespoons all-purpose flour can be used in place of the potato starch.
The cake freezes extremely well.

A Spring Luncheon
EASTER

❧⊙❧⊙❧

Easter is an important Christian holiday celebrated with a bountiful feast. Many elements of this joyful occasion—the pastels of dyed eggs, baskets filled with chocolate storybook bunnies, chicks and lambs, and jelly beans—are favored by all, whether the Easter Bunny brings them or not. Lilies, forsythia, and early blossoms of hyacinths and tulips are abundant during Easter and provide beautiful table settings and hopeful signs of spring for all. It is a perfect time to enjoy the start of the new growing season.

Family traditions play a big part in this celebration, especially for the children. The forty days of Lent (fasting) end on Easter Sunday, and it's a wonderful time for family and friends to gather together for holiday festivities, often after a church service. In the country, there might be an Easter egg hunt or an Easter egg roll on the lawn. We even find places to hide eggs in our city apartments and brownstones, too.

"The night before Easter, there was always a hive of activity centered on my grandparents' porch. The children busied themselves constructing nests for Easter baskets and also painted Easter eggs to further impress the Easter Bunny. After Mass—which, our parents reminded us, was about the true meaning of Easter—we would sit down for the traditional ham. It was served with my great-grandmother's silver and her periwinkle blue-and-white china on a white linen lace-trimmed tablecloth. Further decoration included vases filled with some of the wildflowers we children had picked, surrounded by our hand-painted eggs. While the adults drank rosé Champagne for spring, the children had homemade pink lemonade."

—Stephanie Loeffler

"There is always a personalized dyed egg for each guest, which most likely does double duty as a place card at the lunch. I have even taken Easter candy, tulips, and daffodils and strewn them around the center of the table instead of using a formal centerpiece. Lunch usually starts around 2 p.m."

—Leslie Perkin

THE MENU

Quick Asparagus Hors d'Oeuvres

Penne alla Vodka with Scallops

Nana's Persian Leg of Lamb

Prosciutto and Arugula Salad

Ellie's Double Coconut Layer Cake

Asparagus, lamb, and abundant herbs highlight this menu, a rather eclectic one at that. Warm asparagus hors d'oeuvres are followed by a pasta dish and then a sumptuous braised leg of lamb with fresh chives and mint. Though ham is often the main course for Easter, lamb is the meat of choice in many countries. In this menu, the ham is not ignored but shows up as prosciutto in the arugula salad. A coconut cake that can be decorated with jelly beans or candy eggs or even baked in a lamb-shaped mold is the dessert.

A rosé wine from Spain or Provence would be the ideal accompaniment for this menu, to herald spring and to keep the alcohol moderate. This is Sunday lunch, after all.

ALSO SUGGESTED: *Chilled Minted Zucchini Soup (page 90),*
Smooth Broccoli Soup (page 214), Patsy's Popovers (page 163), Dad's Flemish Pork Stew
(page 66), Chicken Caesar Salad Platter (page 108), Lemon-Fennel Risotto (page 94),
Lemony Tin Box Cheesecake (page 70)

MARY DAVIDSON

Quick Asparagus Hors d'Oeuvres

Hors d'oeuvres made with asparagus have long been
a standard for family cocktail parties.

MAKES ABOUT 18 PIECES

1 BUNCH MEDIUM-THIN ASPARAGUS, ENDS SNAPPED
6 TABLESPOONS MAYONNAISE
2 TABLESPOONS DIJON MUSTARD
⅓ CUP FRESHLY GRATED PARMIGIANO-REGGIANO
1 CUP PANKO (JAPANESE BREAD CRUMBS)
ABOUT 18 ROUNDS MELBA TOAST

Preheat the oven to 400 degrees and line a baking sheet with foil.

Coarsely chop the asparagus, then place in a food processor and pulse until finely chopped. Transfer to a bowl and mix in the mayonnaise, mustard, cheese, and bread crumbs.

Mound the mixture on the melba toast, smoothing the top and edges. Shortly before serving, place on the baking sheet, transfer to the oven, and bake until the tops are lightly browned, about 5 minutes. Remove from the oven, cool briefly, then arrange on a serving plate.

These tidbits are a little easier to handle than whole asparagus spears offered as hors d'oeuvres.

"Sometimes the only thing blooming in New York at Easter is forsythia. I bring it in from the country and spread the tall branches around the apartment."

—Chesie Breen

Penne alla Vodka with Scallops

My dear friend in Beverly Hills, Connie Wald, a quintessential hostess of the Hollywood glamour years, always did the cooking when she entertained. Every time my husband and I came to California to visit our daughter, we stayed with her and she gave a dinner party. And in the land where salad was the standard first course, she always served pasta. This penne alla vodka was everyone's favorite and it is one of many recipes I took home from her house.

Makes 4 to 6 main-course servings, 8 as a first course

12 sea scallops

1 tablespoon extra virgin olive oil

4 tablespoons (½ stick) unsalted butter

2 leeks, cleaned, trimmed, and finely chopped

2 shallots, minced

2 tablespoons dry vermouth

1 cup vodka

½ teaspoon crushed red chile flakes, or to taste

1 cup fresh or canned tomato puree

½ cup crème fraîche or heavy cream

Salt and freshly ground white pepper

1 pound penne

1 tablespoon minced flat-leaf parsley leaves

Trim the small ridge of tendon from the side of each scallop. Pat dry the scallops with paper towels.

Place a large sauté pan over high heat, add the oil, and sear the scallops a few minutes, turning them once, until they are lightly browned. Remove the scallops to a dish. Lower the heat and add the butter. When it has melted, add the leeks and shallots and cook until the vegetables start to soften. Add the vermouth and continue cooking until the vegetables are very tender but not browned. Pour in the vodka, add the chile flakes, and simmer until slightly reduced. Add the tomato puree and crème fraîche and simmer for about 5 minutes, until the mixture is well blended and pink. Season with salt and pepper to taste and add more chile flakes if desired. Set aside until just before serving.

Bring a large pot of salted water to a boil for the penne. Quarter the scallops and add them to the warm sauce in the sauté pan. Add the penne to the boiling water and cook for about 8 minutes, until al dente. Drain well. Fold the penne into the sauce and gently reheat the contents of the pan, stirring, until the ingredients are well combined. Taste and add more salt and pepper if needed.

Divide among individual plates, top with the parsley, and serve.

This dish, an Italian restaurant staple, is made ever so much more interesting with the addition of scallops. Select good-quality sea scallops— diver scallops, if available—that are firm textured.

Nana's Persian Leg of Lamb

An invitation for a meal at Nahid Taghinia-Milani's home is a coveted treasure. Friends and family are seated at round tables for a feast of biblical proportions in celebration of Persian and American holidays, birthdays, anniversaries, or the arrival of her many dear friends from around the world. Her Persian-style leg of lamb is my favorite dish at Easter. In my grown-up years dinner at Nahid's warm and beautiful home always evokes these wonderful childhood memories, not only of her fabulous leg of lamb but of the entire wondrous meal she always prepares with her loving hands. Nana is the affectionate name given her by her grandsons, Alexander and Philip. I once asked them about their favorite restaurant, and they said, "Nana's house." I have to agree.

Makes 8 servings

3 tablespoons extra virgin olive oil

½ leg of lamb, butt end, boned and tied, about 3½ pounds, fat well trimmed

2 medium onions, chopped

4 large cloves garlic, chopped

1 teaspoon salt, or to taste

1 teaspoon freshly ground black pepper

½ teaspoon ground turmeric

1 teaspoon garam masala or good-quality curry powder

2 cups chicken stock

1 tablespoon lemon juice

4 pita breads, split and quartered, or other flatbreads

3 scallions, chopped

½ bunch chives, minced

2 tablespoons minced fresh mint leaves

Heat the oil in a heavy 4-quart casserole over high heat. Place the lamb in the pot and sear it on all sides until the outside is entirely golden brown. Remove the meat to a platter and lower the heat to medium. Add the onions and sauté until golden, about 5 minutes. Stir in the garlic, salt, pepper, turmeric, and garam masala. Cook another minute or so, then stir in the chicken stock and bring to a simmer.

Return the lamb to the pot along with any accumulated juices, put it on a very slow simmer, cover, and cook for about 2½ hours, until the meat is very tender when pierced with a fork.

Transfer the lamb to a cutting board. Snip off the trussing strings.

Increase the heat under the pot to medium-high, add the lemon juice, and cook for about 5 minutes to reduce and thicken the sauce. Check the seasonings and add salt and pepper if needed.

Line a rimmed serving platter with the split quartered pita breads. Use a sharp knife to slice the lamb and arrange the slices over the bread. Spoon the sauce over the meat. Sprinkle on the scallions, chives, and mint and serve.

Slowly braising a leg of lamb results in meat with a delectable succulence, what the French call gigot à la cuillière, or lamb for a spoon, suggesting its tenderness. This is a dish that is extremely user-friendly for the cook, since it can be made earlier in the day and reheated. If you use a casserole that is large enough to hold it, a whole leg of lamb can be prepared to feed a crowd. And leftovers, sliced thin, make delicious sandwiches, in pita bread, of course, with a dressing of yogurt mixed with parsley.

Prosciutto and Arugula Salad

⁓⁕⁓

WE HAVE A LOT OF BIG FAMILY DINNERS, AND AN EASY VARIATION ON
THE BASIC SALAD USING A SIMPLE VINAIGRETTE COMES IN VERY HANDY.
YOU CAN EASILY SCALE UP THE QUANTITIES AND ADD INGREDIENTS YOU LIKE
TOGETHER. SOMETIMES I ADD BOCCONCINI (LITTLE BALLS OF MOZZARELLA).
IF THEY ARE IN SEASON, PEACHES OR MANGOES CAN REPLACE THE TOMATOES.
I ALWAYS WAIT UNTIL THE LAST MINUTE TO ADD THE DRESSING.

MAKES 8 SERVINGS

½ POUND PROSCIUTTO, PREFERABLY IMPORTED,
IN 2 THICK SLICES
¼ CUP RASPBERRY VINEGAR
1 TEASPOON DIJON MUSTARD
½ CUP EXTRA VIRGIN OLIVE OIL
SALT AND FRESHLY GROUND BLACK PEPPER
1 PINT RED OR YELLOW CHERRY, GRAPE, OR PEAR TOMATOES, HALVED
3 BUNCHES OR CONTAINERS BABY ARUGULA OR BABY SPINACH,
RINSED AND DRIED

Dice the prosciutto and set it aside.

In a small bowl, whisk together the vinegar and mustard. Whisk in the oil. Season with salt and pepper to taste.

Place the tomatoes and prosciutto in a salad bowl. Add half the dressing and allow the ingredients to marinate until shortly before serving.

Add the arugula and the remaining dressing, toss, and serve.

*❧ Always rinse and dry the greens, even if the container says ❦
they have been washed. Cutting the small tomatoes in half
instead of using them whole brings out their flavor.*

Ellie's Double Coconut Layer Cake

EVER SINCE SHE WAS A LITTLE GIRL, MY DAUGHTER ELEANOR HAS BEEN AN AVID BAKER. ONE OF HER ALL-TIME FAVORITE RECIPES WAS FOR INA GARTEN'S COCONUT CUPCAKES. NOW AS A YOUNG WOMAN, ELEANOR HAS PERFECTED AND TRANSFORMED HER FAVORITE RECIPE INTO A CAKE.

MAKES 1 LARGE 3-LAYER CAKE

CAKE:

3 STICKS (¾ POUND) UNSALTED BUTTER, AT ROOM TEMPERATURE

3 CUPS ALL-PURPOSE FLOUR

2 TEASPOONS BAKING POWDER

1½ TEASPOONS SALT

1¾ CUPS GRANULATED SUGAR

6 LARGE EGGS

1 TABLESPOON LEMON JUICE

1 16-OUNCE BAG SWEETENED FLAKED COCONUT (ABOUT 2 CUPS)

ICING:

1 POUND CREAM CHEESE, AT ROOM TEMPERATURE

3 STICKS (¾ POUND) UNSALTED BUTTER, AT ROOM TEMPERATURE

1 TEASPOON VANILLA EXTRACT

½ TEASPOON ALMOND EXTRACT

ABOUT 3 CUPS SIFTED CONFECTIONERS' SUGAR

Preheat the oven to 350 degrees. Use a little of the butter to grease three 8-inch cake pans and dust with a little of the flour. Sift the remaining flour with the baking powder and salt into a large bowl and set aside.

Cream the remaining butter with the sugar in a separate bowl. Beat in the eggs one at a time. Add the lemon juice. Fold in the flour mixture and then half the coconut, reserving the rest for decoration. Divide the batter among the pans. Place in the oven and bake for about 25 minutes, until lightly browned, shrinking from the sides, and a cake tester comes out clean.

While the cake layers are cooling, make the icing: Beat the cream cheese and butter together in a large bowl until smooth. Mix in the vanilla and almond extracts. Gradually mix in the confectioners' sugar until the mixture is smooth and spreadable though somewhat soft. Cover and refrigerate for at least 2 hours before using.

Allow the layers to cool in the pans. When completely cooled, invert the layers onto a cutting board or other work surface and frost the top and sides of each layer. Dust with the reserved coconut and stack the layers.

If you own a lamb-shaped mold, by all means use it for this cake, especially for Easter. Decorate the cake with small candy Easter eggs or pastel jelly beans if you like.

A Southern-Style Gathering
DERBY DAY

On the first Saturday in May, all bets are on the Kentucky
Derby—the Run for the Roses. It's a perfect occasion for a
happy gathering and inspires decorations, attire, and the
menu. Whether you are hosting a party in the Bluegrass
State or on Park Avenue, the anticipation leading up to
the event adds exhilaration from the moment guests arrive.
Women are invited to wear spectacular hats, and a betting
pool is certain to add to the fun. All the host needs are
three basic ingredients: a TV tuned into the excitement
at Churchill Downs, hearty Southern-style fare, and
unlimited mint juleps, of course.

❧ THE MENU ❧

CLASSIC MINT JULEPS

TEA SANDWICHES (AS YOU LIKE THEM)

CORNMEAL BATTER CAKES

DAD'S FLEMISH PORK STEW

EVERYTHING CHOPPED SALAD

LEMONY TIN BOX CHEESECAKE

This menu is not 100 percent Southern in its inspiration, but it pushes many of the appropriate buttons, like the juleps, the cornmeal cakes, and the pork stew made with okra and fortified with bourbon. Like many of the celebration menus, it's largely done in advance.

"As a Southern hostess, I'd say to drink a mint julep before your guests arrive and you'll have a fabulous time! I was born and raised in Louisville, Kentucky, and we invite 125 people to celebrate a fine Southern tradition at our home in Connecticut. The party starts around 3 p.m. The mint juleps are the real deal! We make our own simple syrup the night before and have plenty of crushed ice and fresh mint on hand. Our menu is Southern-style, with a country ham shipped from Tennessee and a stunning cheese tray. There's Dixieland music and we all sing 'My Old Kentucky Home' before the race."

— Tammy Harris

ALSO SUGGESTED: *Quick Asparagus Hors d'Oeuvres (page 48), Tailgate Deviled Eggs (page 123), Toasted Cheese Puffs (page 194), Mini Baked Crab Cakes (page 200), Susan's Pork and Clementine Bites (page 204), Prosciutto and Arugula Salad (page 55), Double Salmon Mousse (page 202), Bobby's Crisp Chicken Cutlets (page 124), Beef Stroganoff in a New York Minute (page 164), Fried Green Apples (page 81), Besso's Feathery Pecan Puffs (page 30)*

Classic Mint Juleps

THE KEY HERE IS MAKING THE SIMPLE SYRUP IN ADVANCE AND
USING SPECIAL SHORT SILVER JULEP CUPS.

MAKES 12 DRINKS

I CUP SUGAR
2 BUNCHES FRESH MINT
CRUSHED ICE
I (750-MILLILITER) BOTTLE BOURBON
3 CUPS (24 OUNCES) CHILLED CLUB SODA, OPTIONAL

First, make the sugar syrup (simple syrup). Mix the sugar with 1 cup water in a small saucepan, bring to a simmer, and cook just until the sugar dissolves. Pour into a container, add 1 bunch of the mint, cover, and refrigerate overnight. Remove the mint, draining it well, and discard it.

For each julep, fill a metal julep cup (or an old-fashioned glass) with crushed ice. Pour in 1 tablespoon of the mint syrup and 2 ounces (¼ cup) bourbon. Stir. Add a splash of club soda, if desired, garnish with fresh mint, and serve.

*As a timesaver, keep a container of simple syrup in the refrigerator
to have on hand for cocktails and for sweetening iced tea.*

*"My son's Southern godmother started a tradition when he
was born of giving him one silver mint julep cup on each
birthday so he will have a complete set when he grows up and
something to remind him of his mother's Southern roots!"*
—Elizabeth Fuller

Cornmeal Batter Cakes

AN OLD FAMILY FRIEND WHO LIVES IN LOUISVILLE
GAVE THIS RECIPE TO MY SISTER-IN-LAW.

MAKES 18 CAKES TO SERVE 6

1 CUP CULTURED BUTTERMILK

½ TEASPOON BAKING SODA

1 LARGE EGG, LIGHTLY BEATEN

⅔ CUP WHITE CORNMEAL

¾ TEASPOON SALT

3 TABLESPOONS MELTED UNSALTED BUTTER OR BACON FAT,
PLUS EXTRA FOR GREASING IF NEEDED

SOUR CREAM AND SMOKED SALMON OR SALMON CAVIAR FOR GARNISH, OPTIONAL

Preheat the oven to 200 degrees and line a baking sheet with foil.

Pour the buttermilk into a bowl and stir in the baking soda. Whisk in the egg and gradually whisk in the cornmeal, then the salt and fat and ¼ cup water.

Heat a seasoned griddle, either electric or stove-top, or a cast-iron skillet until quite hot (380 degrees on an electric griddle). Brush with a little of the fat if needed. Spoon tablespoonfuls of the batter onto the griddle or pan to make 5-inch pancakes. Turn each over as they are lightly browned and cook the other side until lightly browned. As they are done, transfer them to the baking sheet and keep them warm in the oven.

Serve the cakes as a side dish or as a first course topped with sour cream and smoked salmon or salmon caviar.

Cultured buttermilk can be difficult to find in shops. Plain yogurt thinned with an equal quantity of skim milk can be substituted. If your griddle or pan is not well seasoned, you might have to brush it with a little fat, probably just for the first batch of cakes. You can also make the cakes very small, silver-dollar size, to use as canapés for smoked salmon or caviar. In this form, they freeze well.

Dad's Flemish Pork Stew

THIS RECIPE WAS GIVEN TO MY PARENTS SOME FORTY YEARS AGO AND
MY DAD HAS REFINED IT OVER THE YEARS. IT'S EASY TO PREPARE THIS
CASSEROLE IN ADVANCE AND IT'S A GREAT BUFFET DISH.

MAKES 6 SERVINGS

¼ POUND SMOKED COUNTRY BACON, DICED
3 POUNDS PORK SHOULDER FOR STEW, WELL TRIMMED
SALT AND FRESHLY GROUND BLACK PEPPER
½ CUP BOURBON
½ CUP ALL-PURPOSE FLOUR
2 TEASPOONS FRESH ROSEMARY LEAVES
1½ CUPS AMBER ALE
ABOUT 2 CUPS CHICKEN STOCK
18 SMALL RED POTATOES, PEELED
7 CARROTS, PEELED AND SLICED DIAGONALLY INTO 2-INCH PIECES
1 CUP FRESH PEAS
18 SMALL OKRA PODS, OPTIONAL
2 TABLESPOONS WORCESTERSHIRE SAUCE

Heat a large enamel cast-iron casserole, add the bacon, and sauté until
browned. Remove the bacon, leaving as much fat as possible in the pot.
Pat dry the pork pieces with paper towels and brown them in the bacon fat.
You may have to do this in a couple of batches. Season with salt and pepper.
Return all the pork to the pot, add the bourbon, and carefully light it with a
long kitchen match. When the flames die down, sprinkle the meat with the
flour and rosemary and stir.

Add the ale and enough stock to barely cover the pork. Bring to a
simmer and cook, covered, for 45 minutes, until the meat is nearly tender.
Meanwhile, parboil the potatoes in a pot of salted water for 15 minutes.

Add the potatoes, carrots, and peas to the pork and simmer for 10 minutes. Add the okra, if using, and simmer 10 minutes more, until all the vegetables are tender. Stir in the Worcestershire sauce. Check the seasoning and add more salt and pepper if needed.

❧ The dish is essentially carbonnades à la flamande, a Belgian beer stew, ❧ given a touch of horse-country personality with the addition of a little bourbon. In winter or fall, small turnips are a fine addition, but for Derby Day, okra gives it an extra Southern accent.

CHESIE BREEN

Everything Chopped Salad

I SERVE A SALAD WITH JUST ABOUT EVERY DINNER MENU. THIS ONE INCLUDES A NUMBER OF COLORFUL VEGETABLES. BECAUSE THEY ARE HARD TO SKEWER WITH A FORK, I DECIDED TO CHOP EVERYTHING INTO LITTLE BITS SO THAT YOU CAN EASILY SLIDE THE SALAD ONTO YOUR FORK. THE BLUE CHEESE HELPS BLEND ALL OF THE INGREDIENTS TOGETHER.

MAKES 6 SERVINGS

2 SMALL ENDIVES, CORED AND CHOPPED

8 ROMAINE LETTUCE LEAVES, CHOPPED

1 CUCUMBER, PEELED, SEEDED, AND CHOPPED

2 CUPS CHOPPED TOMATOES

2 CARROTS, CHOPPED

1 YELLOW BELL PEPPER, CORED AND CHOPPED

4 SCALLIONS, CHOPPED

3 TABLESPOONS WHITE WINE VINEGAR

1 TEASPOON HONEY MUSTARD

6 TABLESPOONS EXTRA VIRGIN OLIVE OIL

¼ POUND BLUE CHEESE, CRUMBLED

Combine the endives, lettuce, cucumber, tomatoes, carrots, bell pepper, and scallions on a large cutting board and chop them all together briefly with a large chef's knife. Transfer the ingredients to a salad bowl.

Whisk the vinegar and mustard together in a medium bowl. Whisk in the oil. Pour over the salad and mix well to coat all the ingredients. Fold in the cheese and serve.

The ingredients can be chopped in a food processor, but for best results, they should be processed one at a time, not all at once before they are combined for the final chopping by hand. The saving grace is that it is not necessary to wash the machine for each item.

Lemony Tin Box Cheesecake

MY MOTHER HAD A TIN BOX OF RECIPES THAT SHE RECEIVED AS A WEDDING GIFT, AND THIS IS ONE OF OUR FAVORITES. MY SISTER KATHERINE STARTED MAKING THIS CAKE, AND NOW I PREPARE IT, TOO. THE TOPPING SETS IT APART.

1½ CUPS GRAHAM CRACKER CRUMBS

¾ CUP PLUS 2 TABLESPOONS SUGAR

FINELY GRATED ZEST AND JUICE OF 1 LEMON

6 TABLESPOONS (¾ STICK) UNSALTED BUTTER, MELTED

3 LARGE EGGS, SEPARATED

1 POUND CREAM CHEESE, SOFTENED

PINCH OF SALT

1 PINT SOUR CREAM

1 TABLESPOON VANILLA EXTRACT

Preheat the oven to 350 degrees.

In a large bowl, mix the crumbs, ¼ cup of the sugar, the lemon zest, and melted butter together. Press into the bottom and partway up the sides of an 8-inch springform cake pan. Place it in the oven and bake for 15 minutes. Remove from the oven and cool. Leave the oven on.

In a large bowl, beat the egg yolks until light, then gradually beat in ½ cup of the sugar until thick and very pale. Stir in the lemon juice. Slowly beat in the cream cheese until smooth.

In another bowl, beat the egg whites with the salt until soft peaks form. Stir a few tablespoons into the cream cheese mixture, then fold in the rest. Pour into the graham cracker crust and return it to the oven. Bake for 30 minutes, or until firm. Remove the cake from the oven, cool completely, then refrigerate until ready to serve.

Combine the sour cream with the remaining 2 tablespoons sugar and the vanilla and spread over the top of the cake. Remove the sides of the pan and serve.

It's easiest to slice a creamy cake like this with a knife dipped in cold water. The cake, without the topping, freezes extremely well.

A Loving Brunch
MOTHER'S DAY

There is nothing more meaningful for a mother than to spend this day with her children. And why not start the day with breakfast in bed? The children, with the help of older siblings and Dad, can lend a hand in preparing the meal and setting a breakfast tray, complete with handmade cards and presents.

This is also a perfect occasion to host a brunch and invite the mothers in the extended families—the grandmothers, great grandmothers, stepmothers, and godmothers, bringing together multiple generations of the women who have shaped our lives.

And while mothers may be treated with a respite from the kitchen on Mother's Day, it's a different story when Father's Day comes around. Then, the man of the house is often given the job of doing the grilling.

❦ THE MENU ❧

POMEGRANATE MIMOSAS

EGGS IN A NEST

FRIED GREEN APPLES

GREAT-GRANDMOTHER CUSHMAN'S BRAN MUFFINS

MARY'S HOUSE OATMEAL COOKIES

This brunch menu, planned for more than just the immediate family, is warm, bright, and springlike, and it has dishes that can be enjoyed by all ages. There is no egg preparation more festive than eggs in a nest. And the recipe for the bran muffins comes from a bona fide great-grandmother.

While the adults sip their pomegranate mimosas, the children can have plain pomegranate juice.

"Put a small bouquet or nosegay—tied with ribbons or in a bud vase—at the place setting of each mother. Even better, make them bouquets of wildflowers gathered by the children. Or, corsages can be a sweet touch to make each mother feel special."
—Chiara Edmands

ALSO SUGGESTED: *Quick Asparagus Hors d'Oeuvres (page 48),*
Tailgate Deviled Eggs (page 123), Cornmeal Batter Cakes (page 64),
Patsy's Popovers (page 163), Mozzarella-Tomato-Basil Frittata (page 107),
Bibb and Avocado Salad (page 241), Ellie's Double Coconut Layer Cake
(page 56), Lemony Tin Box Cheesecake (page 70)

FLORENCE FABRICANT

Pomegranate Mimosas

POMEGRANATE. ELDERFLOWERS. THE EXOTIC JUICES AND LIQUEURS
HAVE GIVEN SO MANY NEW TWISTS TO CLASSIC DRINKS.

MAKES 8 COCKTAILS

2 CUPS POMEGRANATE JUICE, CHILLED
6 OUNCES ELDERFLOWER LIQUEUR
1 BOTTLE SPARKLING WINE, CHILLED

Mix the pomegranate juice and elderflower liqueur in a pitcher. Add the sparkling wine. Pour into Champagne flutes or wineglasses and serve.

❦ Champagne is perfect, but any sparkling wine, ❦
even a modest Prosecco, will do nicely for this drink.

"On Mother's Day little children can make breakfast
with Daddy, things like pancakes from scratch.
We have also had brunch with all the mothers in the
family where we have given everyone little purses with
photos of the children and grandchildren on them,
something special for each one."

—Kathy Thomas

Eggs in a Nest

❦

MY MOTHER USED TO MAKE THESE FOR ME ON HOLLAND RUSKS AND
SHE WOULD SERVE THE EGGS WITH A DELICIOUS CHEESE SAUCE.

MAKES 8 SERVINGS

4 ENGLISH MUFFINS, SPLIT
8 THIN SLICES PROSCIUTTO, COUNTRY HAM, OR SMOKED SALMON
8 LARGE EGGS, SEPARATED
SEA SALT AND FRESHLY GROUND BLACK PEPPER

Preheat the oven to 350 degrees and line a baking sheet with foil.

Lightly toast the English muffins either in a toaster or in the oven on the baking sheet.

Arrange the toasted muffin halves on the baking sheet. Place a slice of ham or salmon on the cut side of each.

In a large bowl, beat the egg whites with a pinch of salt until soft peaks form. Pile the whites on each muffin, covering it (and the ham or salmon) completely. Use the back of a spoon to make a depression in the center of each. Place a yolk in each depression.

Place in the oven and bake for about 15 minutes, until the whites are lightly browned and the yolks are just set. Sprinkle with a little sea salt and pepper and serve immediately.

*❦ The beaten egg whites insulate the ham or salmon from the heat, ❦
keeping this hidden ingredient from overcooking. Children might enjoy these
with a slice of cheese or a slick of jam instead of the ham or salmon.*

Fried Green Apples

FRIED APPLES WERE SOMETHING MY PARENTS ALWAYS MADE FOR BREAKFAST ON SUNDAYS WHEN WE WERE KIDS. MY FATHER IS A GOOD BREAKFAST COOK AND I BELIEVE HE LEARNED THIS RECIPE FROM HIS MOTHER; IT IS A PRETTY COMMON DISH IN VIRGINIA, WHERE WE GREW UP. LEAVING THE SKINS ON MAKES ALL THE DIFFERENCE.

MAKES 8 SERVINGS

3 TABLESPOONS UNSALTED BUTTER

3 LARGE GRANNY SMITH APPLES, CORED,
EACH CUT IN 12 VERTICAL SLICES (WEDGES)

3 TABLESPOONS LIGHT BROWN SUGAR

Melt the butter in a large skillet over medium-high heat. Add the apple slices and sauté a few minutes, turning them as they start to brown. Sprinkle the apples with the brown sugar and continue to sauté and turn them until nicely browned on both sides, then add ¼ cup water and continue to cook, basting, until they are glazed and just tender, about 5 minutes. Arrange on a platter and serve.

The apples can be kept warm in a low oven or slightly undercooked and left in the pan, then briefly reheated.

Great-Grandmother Cushman's Bran Muffins

AFTER FOUR GENERATIONS THESE MUFFINS ARE STILL A FAMILY FAVORITE. EVERYONE, EVEN THE YOUNGEST GRANDCHILDREN, LOVES THEM HOT FROM THE OVEN SERVED WITH WITH GENEROUS AMOUNTS OF BUTTER AND HONEY.

MAKES 12 MUFFINS

1 CUP ALL-PURPOSE FLOUR

1 TEASPOON SALT

1 TEASPOON BAKING SODA

1¾ CUPS WHEAT BRAN

2 TABLESPOONS UNSALTED BUTTER, SOFTENED

¼ CUP SUGAR

1 LARGE EGG

1 CUP CULTURED BUTTERMILK

2 TABLESPOONS MOLASSES

Preheat the oven to 400 degrees. Place fluted papers in a muffin tin to fill 12 cups.

Whisk the flour, salt, and baking soda together in a large bowl. Whisk in the bran.

In a separate bowl, cream the butter, then add the sugar and beat until smooth. Beat in the egg until thick and light. Add the bran mixture in two additions, alternately with the buttermilk. Stir in the molasses.

Spoon the batter into the muffin cups, filling them halfway. Place in the oven and bake for 30 minutes, until a toothpick inserted in the center of a muffin comes out clean. Remove from the oven and cool for a few minutes before removing from the tin and serving.

Pure wheat bran, not the kind that is sold as cereal, is available in health food stores. Oat bran, or a mixture of wheat and oat, can be used as an alternative. Raisins, currants, or chopped pecans can also be added to the batter if you like.

Mary's House Oatmeal Cookies

THESE COOKIES ARE LITERALLY FROM MARY'S HOUSE, AN APARTMENT WHERE I MEET REGULARLY WITH A GROUP OF SMART, FUNNY, AND CREATIVE WOMEN TO DISCUSS THE BUSINESS AT HAND. MARY DURKIN USUALLY SERVES CHICKEN CURRY THAT SHE ORDERS FROM SWIFTY'S, A POPULAR RESTAURANT NEARBY, BUT DESSERT IS ALWAYS HER HOMEMADE COOKIES.

MAKES ABOUT 24 COOKIES

1½ STICKS (6 OUNCES) UNSALTED BUTTER, SOFTENED

⅔ CUP ALL-PURPOSE FLOUR

1 TEASPOON GROUND CINNAMON

½ TEASPOON SALT

½ TEASPOON BAKING SODA

1 CUP LIGHT BROWN SUGAR

½ CUP GRANULATED SUGAR

1 LARGE EGG, LIGHTLY BEATEN

1 TEASPOON VANILLA EXTRACT

2 CUPS QUICK-COOKING OATS

1 CUP RAISINS

Preheat the oven to 350 degrees. Use a little of the butter to grease 2 cookie sheets.

In a large bowl, sift together the flour, cinnamon, salt, and baking soda.

In a separate bowl, cream the butter and gradually beat in the brown sugar, then beat in the granulated sugar. Beat in the egg until the batter is smooth. Beat in the vanilla and 2 tablespoons water. Fold in the flour mixture, then the oats and raisins.

Drop scant tablespoonfuls of the batter onto the baking sheets, placing them about an inch apart. Bake for 8 to 10 minutes until slightly browned. Remove from the oven and cool the cookies on the baking sheets for about 10 minutes, then transfer to wire racks to finish cooling.

If you use nonstick baking sheets or line your baking sheets with parchment paper, you will not have to grease them.

A Milestone to Share
ANNIVERSARY

An anniversary is an occasion to find a theme. Some, like the twenty-fifth, symbolized by silver, are easy. With others, it is meaningful to think about the celebrants and how their interests might suggest a party. A color other than silver, some sport, hobby, or travels might be inspiration for the decorations, entertainment, and even the food.

One thing is certain: A good anniversary party takes planning, often months in advance, especially for a "big" anniversary and one for which some guests might have to travel from afar.

It's important to make an anniversary party a memorable one in every way. And carefully consider how to handle gifts. Some people will welcome them, others would prefer not to acquire more things. Guests might be requested to create poems or other amusements instead of bringing gifts, or to make donations to a charity favored by the guests of honor.

"For the twenty-fifth you can have a whole silver theme on the table, with sparkly glitter sprinkled on the cloths, silver-wrapped chocolate kisses in bowls, and silver chargers under the dinner plates."
—Nicole Limbocker

"Place cards in little silver frames are a nice touch for an anniversary party."
—Coco Kopelman

"For my parents' 40th, we had cocktail napkins printed with all of my parents' little quips about love and marriage. For their 50th we went with their quirky sense of humor and did a pirate theme. The invitations were messages in a bottle with a nautical map to the party inside. For décor, we used two long tables as ships complete with pirates' chests full of glowing jewelry and eye patches, which even the tamest of guests wore!"
— Kathy Thomas

∾ THE MENU ∾

Chilled Minted Zucchini Soup
Derek's Shrimp with Tomato Sauce
Lemon-Fennel Risotto
Perfect Parisian Salad
Festive Warm Berries with Cool Sorbet

An elegant dinner is what is called for here. Like many of the menus, it can be expanded to serve more than just two couples for a bigger celebration. But for more guests, having a waiter or waitress to do the serving and clearing will make it go more smoothly.

Though the menu does not include a celebratory cake, there are several possibilities elsewhere in this book that are suggested in the following list. Champagne for toasting is a given. The rest of the menu can accommodate a rich white wine, a chardonnay from Burgundy for example, or a light red or even a cool rosé wine.

ALSO SUGGESTED: *Quick Asparagus Hors d'Oeuvres (page 48)*,
Double Salmon Mousse (page 202), *Nana's Persian Leg of Lamb (page 52)*,
Lemony Tin Box Cheesecake (page 70), *Ellie's Double Coconut Layer Cake (page 56)*,
Summer Strawberry Shortcake (page 128), *Flourless Dark Chocolate Cake (page 42)*

Chilled Minted Zucchini Soup

MY MOTHER IS A WONDERFUL COOK AND SOME OF THE BEST RECIPES IN HER COLLECTION, LIKE THIS SOUP, ARE THE ONES SHE CREATED. SHE MAKES IT IN THE SUMMER USING FRESH MINT FROM HER GARDEN, WHICH IS SURROUNDED BY A WALL THAT'S ONE HUNDRED YEARS OLD AND IS WHERE SHE LOVES TO ENTERTAIN.

MAKES 4 SERVINGS

1 TEASPOON EXTRA VIRGIN OLIVE OIL

2 TABLESPOONS FINELY CHOPPED ONION

1½ POUNDS ZUCCHINI (ABOUT 5 MEDIUM), TRIMMED AND THINLY SLICED

3 CUPS CHICKEN OR VEGETABLE STOCK

SALT AND FRESHLY GROUND BLACK PEPPER

¾ CUP PLAIN YOGURT

¼ CUP FINELY CHOPPED FRESH MINT LEAVES

Heat the oil in a heavy 3- to 4-quart saucepan over medium heat. Add the onion and one-third of the zucchini. Cook, stirring frequently, until golden, about 5 minutes.

Add the remaining zucchini and the chicken stock, bring to a simmer, and simmer for 15 minutes. Check the seasoning and add salt and pepper if needed. Remove from the heat and set aside until cool. Puree the soup in a food processor or blender in batches, then stir in the yogurt.

Stir in the mint, check the seasoning, and add salt and pepper if needed—remember that the seasonings will not be as strong once the soup is chilled. Cover and refrigerate until cool. Remove from the refrigerator 1 hour before serving.

If summertime brings on the inevitable overabundance of zucchini, use some to make extra batches of this soup and freeze them, adding the mint just before serving.

Derek's Shrimp with Tomato Sauce

I LOVE SHRIMP, ESPECIALLY WHEN COOKED QUICKLY AND SERVED WITH JUST A FEW OTHER FLAVORS SO THE TASTE OF THE SHRIMP SHINES THROUGH. THIS RECIPE WAS GIVEN TO ME BY JOSEPH VERNER REED BACK IN THE 1960S WHEN I WAS WORKING FOR THE AMERICAN SHAKESPEARE THEATER IN STRATFORD, CONNECTICUT. I NEEDED A SIMPLE MAIN COURSE FOR DINNER, AND THIS RECIPE FILLED THE BILL. IT'S DELICIOUS SERVED WITH RICE.

MAKES 4 SERVINGS

2 TABLESPOONS UNSALTED BUTTER

1 TABLESPOON EXTRA VIRGIN OLIVE OIL

1 POUND LARGE SHRIMP (ABOUT 30), SHELLED AND DEVEINED

1 CLOVE GARLIC, MINCED

3 TABLESPOONS TOMATO PASTE

1 BAY LEAF

2 TABLESPOONS LEMON JUICE

2 TABLESPOONS DRY SHERRY

¾ CUP HEAVY CREAM, PLUS MORE IF NEEDED

SALT AND FRESHLY GROUND BLACK PEPPER

1 TABLESPOON FINELY MINCED FLAT-LEAF PARSLEY LEAVES

Melt the butter in a large skillet over medium heat. Add the oil and raise the heat to medium-high. Add the shrimp and sauté, turning them, just until they turn pink, about 2 minutes. Remove the shrimp from the pan.

Add the garlic, stir, and then add the tomato paste. Stir again and add the bay leaf, lemon juice, sherry, and cream. Bring to a simmer, season the sauce with salt and pepper, and add a little more cream if needed. Return the shrimp to the pan, heat through, and serve, garnished with parsley.

❧ These days seafood must be labeled as to country of origin. It's a good thing because ❧ some countries do not farm their shrimp as sustainably as others. Try to find wild shrimp from Florida and the Gulf of Mexico. Farmed shrimp from those areas are also a good choice.

Lemon–Fennel Risotto

THIS WAS A SPUR-OF-THE-MOMENT EXPERIMENT THAT I TRIED, KNOWING I WANTED LEMON RISOTTO BUT NOT SURE WHERE TO GO FROM THERE. I MADE IT WITH A SMALL AMOUNT OF RICE AND CHICKEN STOCK IN ONE SAUCEPAN AND WITH VEGETABLE STOCK IN THE OTHER AND KEPT EXPERIMENTING WITH DIFFERENT SPICES. I REALLY LIKED IT BEST WITH VEGETABLE STOCK, THOUGH YOU CAN USE CHICKEN STOCK IF YOU PREFER. SOMETIMES THE JOURNEY IS HALF THE FUN!

MAKES 4 SERVINGS

2 TABLESPOONS EXTRA VIRGIN OLIVE OIL
½ CUP FINELY CHOPPED ONION
½ CUP FINELY CHOPPED FRESH FENNEL
GRATED ZEST AND JUICE OF 1 LEMON
1 CUP ARBORIO RICE
⅓ CUP DRY WHITE WINE
ABOUT 3 CUPS WELL-SEASONED VEGETABLE OR CHICKEN STOCK,
KEPT AT A SIMMER
SALT AND FRESHLY GROUND BLACK PEPPER
1 TABLESPOON MINCED FENNEL FRONDS

Heat the oil in a 3-quart saucepan over low heat. Add the onion and chopped fennel and sauté until softened but not browned, about 5 minutes. Stir in the lemon zest, then the rice. Cook, stirring, for about 5 minutes, until the rice turns opaque. Add the wine and the lemon juice and cook, stirring, until the liquid is nearly absorbed.

Add ½ cup of the stock and cook, stirring, until it is nearly absorbed, then continue to add stock, ½ cup at a time, until the rice is just tender and the liquid is creamy, about 15 minutes. Season with salt and pepper to taste and remove from the heat.

Just before serving, stir the rice mixture, add a little more stock, and heat through. Fold in the fennel fronds and serve.

There is a great deal about making risotto that might intimidate a novice cook. One is told to stir it constantly and never make it in advance and reheat it. But guess what? Neither warning has to be heeded. The key is to adjust the heat so the ingredients simmer in a lively fashion. Then you can stir it from time to time, particularly after adding more liquid. And you can set it aside, covered, when about two-thirds of the liquid has been added, then gently reheat it and finish cooking the rice in about 5 minutes.

Perfect Parisian Salad

I WAS SERVED THIS SALAD IN A DARLING LITTLE BISTRO ON MY VERY FIRST TRIP TO PARIS THIRTY YEARS AGO, AND I HAVE BEEN MAKING IT FOR DINNER PARTIES EVER SINCE.

MAKES 4 SERVINGS

1 golden Delicious apple, peeled, cored, and diced

1 head endive, quartered lengthwise,
core removed, and slivered vertically

Juice of 1 lemon

1 cup walnut halves, toasted and chopped

1 tablespoon white wine vinegar

1 teaspoon Dijon mustard

¼ cup extra virgin olive oil

Salt and freshly ground pepper

1 head Boston lettuce, trimmed

Place the apple and endive in a salad bowl and toss with the lemon juice. Fold in the walnuts.

Whisk together the vinegar and mustard in a small bowl. Whisk in the oil. Pour over the apple and endive mixture and toss. Season with salt and pepper to taste. Just before serving, tear the lettuce in bite-size pieces, add them to the salad, toss again to coat with the dressing, and serve.

Mixing the apples and endive with the lemon juice and dressing keeps them from turning brown. And the authenticity of the recipe is verified by its use of a golden Delicious apple, a favorite of French chefs. But another type of apple, like Fuji, also can be used.

Festive Warm Berries with Cool Sorbet

I RECEIVED THIS RECIPE FROM A GREAT FRIEND WHO USED TO BE A FOOD EDITOR FOR THE SUNDAY *New York Times Magazine*. SHE BEDAZZLED ME WITH THE SIMPLICITY OF IT ALL. I LIKE TO SERVE IT IN THE SUMMER, AND NOW I BEDAZZLE MY GUESTS! SERVE IT IN A SORBET DISH OR A SAUCER-STYLE CHAMPAGNE GLASS FOR A SPECIAL PRESENTATION.

MAKES 4 SERVINGS

1 TABLESPOON UNSALTED BUTTER

3 TABLESPOONS LIGHT BROWN SUGAR

2 CUPS BLUEBERRIES OR A MIXTURE OF BLUEBERRIES AND RASPBERRIES

2 TABLESPOONS GIN OR RASPBERRY EAU DE VIE, OPTIONAL

1 PINT RASPBERRY SORBET

½ CUP CRÈME FRAÎCHE, OPTIONAL

Melt the butter in a medium skillet over medium heat. Add the sugar and swirl it until it melts. Fold in the berries and cook them just until they start to collapse and give up their liquid.

Remove from the heat and set aside. Stir in the gin or eau de vie, if using. Just before serving, slightly rewarm the fruit. Place scoops of sorbet in large wineglasses. Spoon the warm berry mixture over the sorbet and top with a dollop of crème fraîche if you like.

Blueberries and gin pair beautifully. Blackberries can also be used, but not strawberries, as they do not stand up well to cooking.

"A seated meal requires diligence and thoughtfulness on the part of the hostess. Try to seat together people who may not know each other but have a common interest or mutual friends. You want there to be a bridge for conversation, and it's fun to meet new people in an enjoyable setting."
—Muffie Potter Aston

A Patriotic Buffet
FOURTH OF JULY

What better time of the year to celebrate than the Fourth
of July! A waterside locale always seems to provide the
perfect backdrop to this meaningful and joyful holiday.
Small town parades and fireworks are the showstoppers
that make summer memories year after year. In New York
City, many parties are planned in apartments with a river
view—all the better to see the fireworks that light up the sky
over the East River and the Hudson. In Southampton after
the traditional Fourth of July Parade, many families host
poolside picnics at home. For others, a seasonal treat is the
classic clambake on the beach as the sun is setting.

"Decorating is achieved simply with bright white plates, blue cloths, and red napkins with clusters of miniature flags in small glass vases. And red votives add a festive glow."

— Coco Kopelman

"A family friend used to dress in full colonial garb and read the Declaration of Independence. We then sang 'The Star Spangled Banner' while waving sparklers. It was such a memorable sight. For our family parties now, we assign different parts of the Declaration of Independence for the children and veterans alike to recite. It gives meaning to the celebration across all generations."

— Jessie Araskog

"I became engaged on Shell Beach on Shelter Island and from that day on, shells have been a central part of my life. The place cards at my wedding were large sand dollars and many of the guests still have them as mementos and décor in their homes. I incorporate shells into all of my entertaining at our summer home. I have an assortment of various sized scallop shells which hold hors d'oeuvres and first course entrées nicely."

—Catherine Carey

THE MENU

South Texas Watermelon Margaritas

Mozzarella-Tomato-Basil Frittata

Chicken Caesar Salad Platter

Summer Bean Salad

Aunt Sandy's Cobbler

Fourth of July represents the first flush of summer, when the farm stands and markets have ripe berries, peaches, cherries, and, often, the earliest corn and field tomatoes of the season. It is a moment to celebrate this bounty, too. A buffet party can be a lunch, even a picnic, or an early evening event before heading to a viewing station to admire the din and dazzle of fireworks after dark. This menu can serve twelve, halved to serve six, or even doubled for a big party.

Having a generous pitcher of margaritas is a good way to start the party, but red and white wine, juices, soft drinks, and water should also be supplied. Whether to have a full bar in addition is up to you, but that might require hiring a bartender.

ALSO SUGGESTED: *Tailgate Deviled Eggs (page 123), Farm Stand Gazpacho (page 140), Texas Corn Pudding (page 127), Summertime Blueberry Squares (page 152), Summer Strawberry Shortcake (page 128)*

STEPHANIE LOEFFLER

South Texas Watermelon Margaritas

GROWING UP IN SOUTH TEXAS INCLUDED MANY HAPPY SUMMERS AT OUR RANCH. AFTER A LONG AFTERNOON RIDING THE FENCE LINE ON HORSEBACK WITH GRANDPA, WE WOULD RETURN HOME MOSQUITO-BITTEN BUT SMILING AND SUNBURNED, TO BE GREETED BY GRANDMA'S COLD SWEET ICED TEA AND HUGE SLICES OF WATERMELON SET OUT ON THE PORCH. THIS COCKTAIL, A GROWN-UP VERSION OF THAT MEMORY, IS HOW WE NOW CELEBRATE THE START OF THE LONG, FESTIVE SUMMER SEASON.

MAKES 12 DRINKS

1 SMALL ROUND SEEDLESS WATERMELON
1 CUP FRESH LIME JUICE
3 CUPS SILVER TEQUILA
¾ CUP COINTREAU

Quarter the watermelon and remove the red flesh. Chop it and place in a food processor. Puree the watermelon, then transfer it to a pitcher of ice. Add the remaining ingredients, mix well, and pour into cocktail glasses straight up or on the rocks.

Though watermelon juice is sold in some stores, it's best to use a fresh watermelon and make the puree from scratch. Seedless melons simplify the task.

"Put crackers—the party favor that you snap—on the tables. We bring out crackers for every occasion."
—Nicole Limbocker

Mozzarella-Tomato-Basil Frittata

I CREATED THIS RECIPE FOR A BRUNCH WITH FRIENDS IN OUR APARTMENT TO WATCH A DUKE UNIVERSITY BASKETBALL GAME. IT IS MEANT TO BE A TWIST ON THE USUAL PIZZA. I'M TERRIBLE AT FLIPPING OMELETS, AND I HAD TWELVE PEOPLE TO SERVE, SO A COUPLE OF FRITTATAS MADE SENSE. I LET THE CHEESE GET GOOD AND MELTED, AND I SERVE THE FRITTATAS ON CERAMIC PLATTERS WE BOUGHT ON OUR HONEYMOON. THE RECIPE IS WONDERFUL FOR SUMMER ENTERTAINING.

MAKES 12 SERVINGS

12 LARGE EGGS
½ CUP WHOLE MILK
2 TABLESPOONS EXTRA VIRGIN OLIVE OIL
4 LARGE RIPE TOMATOES, PEELED AND SLICED
1 POUND FRESH OR SMOKED MOZZARELLA, DICED
2 TABLESPOONS SLIVERED BASIL LEAVES
SALT AND FRESHLY GROUND BLACK PEPPER

Preheat the broiler.

In a large bowl, beat the eggs with the milk.

Pour 1 tablespoon of the oil into a very large ovenproof skillet, or use 2 skillets with half the ingredients in each. Place over medium heat on the stovetop and pour in the egg mixture. Scatter the tomatoes, cheese, and basil over the eggs. Season with salt and pepper to taste.

When the bottom just begins to brown, place the skillet under the broiler just until the top is set, a minute or less. Remove from the oven and use a large spatula to transfer the frittata to a serving platter. Cool about 10 minutes, cut into wedges, and serve.

Fresh ripe tomatoes and high-quality fresh mozzarella (or, if you prefer, smoked mozzarella) are the keys to the success of this recipe. A well-seasoned cast-iron skillet works extremely well.

Chicken Caesar Salad Platter

This recipe came from my sister, Lisa. The salad was served at the bridal shower that she and Kristin Biddle had for me at Kristin's beautiful home in Brooklyn Heights, and making it always brings back the best memories.

Makes 12 servings

2 cloves garlic, chopped

⅔ cup extra virgin olive oil

16 canned anchovies, drained

2 teaspoons Worcestershire sauce

1 teaspoon salt

2 teaspoons dry mustard

½ teaspoon freshly ground black pepper

2 large eggs

Juice of 2 lemons

⅔ cup grated Parmigiano-Reggiano cheese

3 pounds boneless, skinless chicken breasts (about 6)

2 heads romaine lettuce, cores removed

1 cup unseasoned croutons

Place the garlic, oil, anchovies, Worcestershire sauce, salt, mustard, pepper, eggs, lemon juice, and cheese in a blender. Add ⅓ cup water and blend until smooth.

Place the chicken in a dish, add ¼ cup of the dressing, turn the chicken to coat, and marinate for about 1 hour. Shortly before serving, grill the chicken on an outdoor grill or in a grill pan on the stove or under the broiler, turning it once, until just cooked through, about 15 minutes. Remove to a cutting board.

Shred the lettuce into a large bowl. Add the croutons and the remaining dressing and toss. Transfer the salad to a large platter or shallow serving bowl. Slice the chicken ½ inch thick, arrange the slices over the salad, and serve.

Mixing the dressing in a blender is effective and convenient.
And the dressing is a fine marinade for chicken—or seafood—
even when no Caesar salad accompanies it.

Summer Bean Salad

My mother concocted this recipe, and now it is a summer staple.
Its fresh seasonal ingredients pack a lot of flavor.

Makes 10 to 12 servings

2 cups dried black beans or 2 (15-ounce) cans black beans,
drained and rinsed

4 cups chicken stock, optional

2 cups cooked corn kernels (from 3 to 4 cobs)

1 large green bell pepper, cored, seeded, and finely chopped

1 medium jícama, peeled and diced (about 2 cups)

⅓ cup finely chopped red onion

Juice of 3 limes

¼ cup extra virgin olive oil

Salt and freshly ground black pepper to taste

½ teaspoon cayenne, or to taste

1 bunch cilantro, stems removed, leaves chopped

If using dried beans, the night before, soak the beans in water to cover by 2 inches. Drain them the next day. Place in a saucepan, cover with 4 cups fresh water or the chicken stock, bring to a simmer, and cook for 1 hour, or until tender. Drain.

Place the beans in a large bowl. Add the remaining ingredients and mix well. Set aside to marinate for about 4 hours at room temperature. Check the seasonings, adding salt and pepper if needed, and serve.

Believe it or not, when it comes to dried beans, there is a freshness factor. If you plan to use dried beans rather than canned, be sure to buy fresh-looking packages—some will have a "use by" date—and do not leave them in your pantry for years on end. Fresher dried beans will cook to creamy smoothness. And make sure not to undercook them—taste them to make sure they are tender.

Aunt Sandy's Cobbler

My Aunt Sandy is wonderfully Southern. My mother would make her cobbler all summer long, especially for the Fourth of July and summer birthdays. It has lots of fruit—my favorite is peaches—and not too much crust. You can be creative and mix it up with a variety of fruits.

Makes 12 servings

1½ sticks (6 ounces) unsalted butter, softened

1½ cups all-purpose flour

1¼ teaspoons baking powder

½ teaspoon salt

2 cups sugar, plus more for sprinkling

2 large eggs

10 peaches, peeled, pitted, and sliced, or 10 nectarines, pitted and sliced

1 pint blueberries or blackberries

Whipped cream, crème fraîche, or vanilla ice cream for serving, optional

Preheat the oven to 300 degrees. Use a little of the butter to grease a large baking dish, at least 9 by 13 inches.

Whisk the flour, baking powder, and salt together in a large bowl.

Cream the remaining butter in a separate bowl. Beat in 1½ cups of the sugar, then beat in the eggs one at a time. Stir in the flour mixture to make a thick batter.

Mix the fruit with the remaining ½ cup sugar and spread in the baking dish. Drop the batter by spoonfuls over the top. Sprinkle with sugar. Place in the oven and bake for about 1 hour, until the topping is golden brown and the fruit is bubbling. Remove from the oven and cool at least 30 minutes before serving. The cobbler can be reheated. Serve warm or at room temperature with whipped cream, crème fraîche, or vanilla ice cream if you like.

Though this dessert represents summer at its most glorious, early autumn's plums, apples, pears, and even quinces, perhaps mixed with dried fruit that has been soaked to soften it, can also be used.

A Bash for All Ages
CHILDREN'S BIRTHDAY PARTY

A children's party in summer is a blessing because it can usually be held outdoors. The most important consideration is that the little ones be kept busy and entertained. It is not necessary to hire professionals to make this overly elaborate—imagination can go a long way. A treasure hunt in the backyard, on the beach, or even in a park can keep young childen occupied. And their finds—pennies, tiny plastic toys, whistles—will provide them with bags of party favors. Make it a picnic and bring out platters or baskets brimming with foods like those we have suggested (which can be prepared in advance and do not need to be served hot). This will give you time to share the summertime festivities along with the children.

"My Swedish sister-in-law introduced us to one of her family traditions — serving birthday cake for breakfast on the morning of the actual birthday. Adults like this too!"
—Barbara McLaughlin

"Birthday parties at home are the most fun. You can put craft paper on tables for the kids to decorate to keep them busy as everyone is arriving. But you must always have something for the adults—hors d'oeuvres, crudités, and wine."
—Maryanne Greenfield

"Think about renting low tables and chairs for the children."
—Nicole Limbocker

❧ THE MENU ☙

The Mecox
Children's Party Punch
Tailgate Deviled Eggs
Bobby's Crisp Chicken Cutlets
Texas Corn Pudding
Summer Strawberry Shortcake
Kathleen's Wheat-Free Fudge Brownies

This is a kid-friendly menu that will also satisfy the adults: a bright punch, deviled eggs, chicken "fingers," and a corn pudding that's a close cousin to "mac-and-cheese." Strawberry shortcake is another crowd-pleaser, waiting for birthday candles.

And for those with wheat allergies, the brownies are a treat they can enjoy (and the chicken cutlets can be breaded with cornmeal instead of flour). On that subject, it pays to inquire of parents whether there are any special dietary considerations, and, if necessary, request that the parents bring special food their children can safely enjoy.

ALSO SUGGESTED: *South Texas Watermelon Margaritas (page 104), Chicken Caesar Salad Platter (page 108), Mother's Spiked Meatloaf (page 147), Summertime Blueberry Squares (page 152), Aunt Sandy's Cobbler (page 112)*

The Mecox

THE FIRST SUMMER MY HUSBAND AND I WERE DATING WE RENTED A GREAT
HOUSE IN THE HAMPTONS WITH FRIENDS. THE HOUSE WAS PERFECT FOR
ENTERTAINING LARGE GROUPS, WHICH WE DID JUST ABOUT EVERY WEEKEND.
THIS WAS THE SIMPLEST, MOST REFRESHING COCKTAIL WE COULD WHIP UP
QUICKLY AND IN LARGE QUANTITIES, AND SPRIGS OF FRESH-CUT MINT FROM
THE GARDEN MAKE IT ALL THE MORE SUMMERY AND SPECIAL. TO THIS DAY
EVERYONE WHO VISITED US IN THIS HOUSE RE-CREATES THIS COCKTAIL.

MAKES 6 TO 8 TALL DRINKS

½ CUP SUGAR

½ CUP LEMON JUICE

½ CUP LIMONCELLO

1 ½ CUPS VODKA

2 ½ CUPS SPARKLING WATER

FRESH MINT SPRIGS

Mix the sugar with ½ cup water in a small saucepan. Place over medium heat, bring to a simmer, and simmer just until the sugar has dissolved. Set aside to cool. This is simple syrup (see page 62).

Place the lemon juice and ½ cup water in a pitcher of ice. Stir in the limoncello. Stir in ¼ cup of the sugar syrup and add the vodka.

Strain into tall glasses filled with fresh ice. Add sparkling water and mint sprigs and serve.

Limoncello is a liqueur, traditionally from Capri, that gets its flavor from an infusion of lemon peel.

Children's Party Punch

THIS WAS A FAVORITE AT HOLIDAY PARTIES FOR CHILDREN WHEN I WAS GROWING UP.
MY PARENTS WOULD ALWAYS HAVE A SPECIAL PUNCH BOWL JUST FOR THE KIDS.
NOW MY FRIENDS ALL SERVE IT FOR THEIR CHILDREN.

MAKES 8 SERVINGS

1 QUART SORBET, A SINGLE FLAVOR OR A MIXTURE

24 OUNCES GINGER ALE, OTHER SOFT DRINK, OR SPARKLING WATER

1 PINT BLUEBERRIES

Place the sorbet in a bowl. Pour the soda over the sorbet and add the blueberries. Use a ladle to spoon into small cups or glasses.

At a party for children, servings of this punch may be one occasion for relaxing the general rule of gracious entertaining—that of not using paper or plastic cups. Colorful children's party ware will do just fine.

"Plastic glasses are mostly for children. This is the time to use them—at picnics and around the pool or on the beach. I also keep plastic glasses in reserve should I run out of glasses at a big cocktail party."

—Susan Burke

Tailgate Deviled Eggs

⁓

MY GRANDMOTHER NANA MADE UP THIS RECIPE AND IT HAS SINCE BEEN A STAPLE AT JUST ABOUT EVERY SPECIAL OCCASION IN THE POTTER HOUSEHOLD. THE DEVILED EGGS LOOK SO PRETTY ON A SILVER TRAY OR PLATTER OR IN A BASKET, WITH PARSLEY SPRINKLED AROUND THE EDGES AND CHIVES SCATTERED ON TOP.

MAKES 8 TO 12 SERVINGS

12 HARD-COOKED EGGS
¼ CUP MAYONNAISE
¼ CUP BOTTLED CHILI SAUCE OR 2 TABLESPOONS KETCHUP
PLUS TABASCO SAUCE TO TASTE
¼ CUP MINCED CHIVES
SALT AND FRESHLY GROUND PEPPER TO TASTE

Cut each egg in half and remove the yolks to a bowl. Mash the yolks. Add the remaining ingredients, reserving 1 tablespoon of the chives for garnish, and mash until smooth. Pile the yolk mixture back into the whites. Arrange the egg halves on a platter, sprinkle each with a bit of the reserved chives, and refrigerate until ready to serve.

Successful hard-cooked eggs are not as easy as boiling water. When properly prepared, the white will be firm but not rubbery, and the yolk will be cooked through but still moist and will not have an ugly gray ring around it. Some authorities recommend boiling eggs for 15 minutes for hard cooked. Julia Child's method is based on one developed by the Georgia Egg Board: Place the eggs in a pan large enough for them to be covered with water to a depth of 2 inches. Bring to a boil, remove the pan from the heat, cover it, and leave for 17 minutes. Then place the eggs in a bowl of ice and water for 2 minutes to chill them quickly. This will make them easier to peel, as the cold causes the whites to shrink from the shell.

Bobby's Crisp Chicken Cutlets

I AM SO PLEASED TO BE ABLE TO SHARE THIS RECIPE THAT HAS BEEN DELIGHTING OUR FAMILY FOR YEARS. IT COMES FROM ROBERT (BOB) ANDREW WALSH, WHO IS MARRIED TO MY SISTER ELLEN. BOB GREW UP IN BOSTON, AS PART OF A LARGE FAMILY. HIS LOVE OF COOKING CAME FROM HIS MOTHER WHO RAISED HER SONS WITH OLD-FASHIONED YANKEE VALUES. IN BOB'S OWN WORDS, "OUR MOTHER MADE US ALL TAKE PART IN FOOD PREPARATION AND CLEANUP AFTER DINNER. THIS IS WHERE MY LOVE OF COOKING BEGAN."

FOR A SIMPLE WEEKNIGHT DINNER, I LOVE TO SERVE THE CRISPY CHICKEN CUTLETS WITH RICE PILAF, FRESH ASPARAGUS, A LOVELY BIBB LETTUCE SALAD, AND SOME TOASTED PITA BREAD WITH BUTTER AND DILL SPRINKLED ON TOP. AS AN ALTERNATIVE TO DINNER, THESE TASTY MORSELS, CUT INTO BITE-SIZE PIECES, ARE GREAT SERVED LIKE CHICKEN NUGGETS WITH A NICE HONEY MUSTARD SAUCE. THIS IS A VERY APPEALING HORS D'OEUVRE FOR ALL AGES, EVEN THOSE WHO ARE FINICKY!

MAKES 8 SERVINGS

2 POUNDS SKINLESS, BONELESS CHICKEN BREASTS,
POUNDED TO ½ INCH THICK

¾ CUP ALL-PURPOSE OR WHOLE WHEAT FLOUR, OR A MIXTURE

SALT AND FRESHLY GROUND BLACK PEPPER

2 LARGE EGGS

2 CUPS BREAD CRUMBS MADE FROM 10 OUNCES COUNTRY BREAD,
CRUSTS REMOVED

2 TEASPOONS MINCED DILL OR OTHER HERB

2 TABLESPOONS EXTRA VIRGIN OLIVE OIL

6 TABLESPOONS (¾ STICK) UNSALTED BUTTER

LEMON WEDGES

Cut the chicken into strips about 1 inch by 2 inches. Season the flour with salt and pepper to taste and spread over a dinner plate. Beat the eggs with 2 tablespoons water in a shallow bowl. Place the bread crumbs on another plate and mix with the dill.

Dust the chicken strips with flour, dip in the egg, then coat with the bread crumbs. Arrange them on a platter, cover with plastic wrap, and refrigerate for at least 30 minutes and up to 2 hours.

Heat the oil and butter in a large skillet over medium-high heat until the butter is melted. Fry the chicken strips, turning each once, until lightly browned. Transfer to a serving platter and serve, either warm or at room temperature, with lemon wedges.

In place of crumbs made from country bread, you can use panko, coarse Japanese bread crumbs. Whole grain panko is a good choice.

❧ Depending on the taste of your guests, this dish can be made with ❧
stronger cheese, like sharp cheddar or Asiago, or a mixture of the two,
and with layers of green chiles added after each layer of cheese.

Texas Corn Pudding

∽⌒∾

I WAS GIVEN THIS FAMILY RECIPE BY MY FRIEND MAUD CABOT FROM BOSTON. WE MET IN CALIFORNIA AT AN ASHRAM, AND AS WE HIKED IN THE SANTA MONICA MOUNTAINS OUR CONVERSATIONS INEVITABLY TURNED TO FOOD. MAUD SENT ME THIS WONDERFUL RECIPE AND I LOVE TO MAKE IT IN SUMMER. I ALSO SERVE IT AT DINNER PARTIES IN THE FALL WHEN WE REUNITE WITH OUR FRIENDS AND SHARE OUR SUMMER EXPERIENCES.

MAKES 8 SERVINGS

2 TABLESPOONS UNSALTED BUTTER

2 LARGE EGGS

1 CUP YELLOW CORNMEAL

1 TEASPOON BAKING SODA

1 TEASPOON SALT

3 CUPS FRESHLY GRATED CORN (FROM 4 TO 5 EARS)

1/3 CUP HEAVY CREAM

1 1/2 CUPS MILK

1 POUND SHREDDED MONTEREY JACK

2 (4-OUNCE) CANS GREEN CHILES, DRAINED AND CHOPPED

Preheat the oven to 350 degrees.

Place the butter in a 2-quart ceramic casserole dish and place in the oven to melt the butter. Remove from the oven and set aside.

Beat the eggs in a large bowl. Beat in the cornmeal, baking soda, and salt. Stir in the corn, cream, and milk. Pour one-third of the batter into the casserole and top with one-third of the cheese. Repeat with half of the remaining batter, half of the remaining cheese and the rest of the batter. Top with the remaining cheese. Cover loosely with foil and bake for about 35 minutes, until set and golden. Serve warm, with the chiles on the side.

Summer Strawberry Shortcake

This cake looks beautiful on a buffet table. It is the perfect way to end a summer birthday party, or you could decorate it with blueberries for a festive Fourth of July cake.

Makes 8 or more servings

3 cups all-purpose flour

1 teaspoon baking soda

¾ teaspoon baking powder

½ teaspoon salt

About ½ cup sugar

⅛ teaspoon cream of tartar

2 sticks (½ pound) unsalted butter, chilled and diced

7 to 8 tablespoons cultured buttermilk

4 cups strawberries, sliced, plus whole berries for garnish

1½ cups heavy cream

3 tablespoons confectioners' sugar

1 teaspoon vanilla extract

Preheat the oven to 425 degrees.

Place the flour, baking soda, baking powder, salt, 3 tablespoons of the sugar, and the cream of tartar in a food processor and pulse to blend. Add the butter and pulse until the mixture is mealy. Transfer the mixture to a bowl, sprinkle on the buttermilk, and mix with a fork just until the ingredients come together to form a dough. Let the dough rest a couple of minutes, then knead it a few times, until it is smooth. Divide it in half.

Pat each portion of the dough into an 8-inch round cake pan. Place in the oven and bake for 10 to 12 minutes, until golden. Remove from the oven and invert the cakes onto racks to cool.

Place the strawberries in a bowl and sweeten them to taste with the remaining sugar.

"Summer has always been a time for family birthdays and anniversaries: We have six in July and six in August. So a constant 'happy tous les temps' atmosphere prevails for two months, with beach picnics and as much outdoor eating as weather permits."

—Leslie Perkin

When the cakes have cooled, whip the cream, gradually adding the confectioners' sugar. When soft peaks form, add the vanilla and whip until firm peaks form.

Place one of the cakes on a cake plate. Spread a little of the whipped cream on top. Top with half of the berries. Place the second cake on top and gently press down. Cover the top with the remaining berries and frost the entire cake with the rest of the whipped cream. Refrigerate for 1 to 3 hours before serving. Garnish with the whole berries and serve.

❀ Strawberry shortcake, for traditionalists, is made with biscuits. ❀ But there is another faction that prefers layers of tender sponge cake. To satisfy both tastes, these cake layers are halfway between biscuit and sponge cake. The cake layers can be made in advance and frozen.

Kathleen's Wheat-Free Fudge Brownies

Back in the early seventies in Southampton we would visit Kathleen King's family farm, where we would buy our fresh vegetables, eggs, and flowers and our favorite chocolate chip cookies that were baked by Kathleen when she was a young girl. Kathleen went on to open a bake shop, and my home was filled with guests who loved her sweets. We served them on the terrace and took them to the beach. I smile when I see Tate's cookies—the brand name she now uses, in honor of her dad—in markets all over the country. Fresh batches of baked goods coming out of her ovens in Southampton still remind me of wonderful memories of her dad's farm and the glorious days of summers past.

Makes 16 brownies

6 tablespoons (¾ stick) salted butter

¾ cup almond flour or very finely ground almonds

¼ teaspoon baking soda

¼ teaspoon salt

2 cups semisweet chocolate bits (about 12 ounces)

1 teaspoon vanilla extract

⅔ cup sugar

2 large eggs, lightly beaten

1 cup fresh raspberries

Preheat the oven to 350 degrees and use a little of the butter to grease a 9-inch square baking pan.

Mix the almond flour, baking soda, and salt together in a small bowl. Place the chocolate and vanilla in a large bowl.

In a saucepan, melt the remaining butter with the sugar and 2 tablespoons water. Bring to a simmer, pour over the chocolate in the bowl, and stir until the chocolate has melted. Add the eggs, beating well. Fold in the almond flour mixture, then fold in the raspberries. Spread in the baking pan.

Place in the oven and bake for about 30 minutes, until fairly firm on top and a cake tester does not come out perfectly clean. Remove from the oven and cool, then refrigerate before cutting.

Like the Flourless Dark Chocolate Cake (page 42), these brownies will have the perfect texture if they are removed from the oven when a cake tester does not come out perfectly clean—moistness is the key.

"I love any occasion to give presents to friends and family. An early summer celebration is a great time to put one of my favorite books at everyone's seat at the table, for their summer reading. I also love using lottery tickets as place cards."

—Patsy Warner

A Picnic by the Water
LABOR DAY

Warm mid-August weather is likely to linger for weeks, but at Labor Day, summer's closing bell inexorably sounds. School starts again. Shoes will replace flip-flops. And the calendar will soon begin to fill with fall and winter events, obligations, and celebrations.

But giving summer a proper send-off is a tradition worth maintaining. It allows for farewell gatherings of summer friends who may not figure as regularly in one's city social life. And it offers a final chance to enjoy truly informal entertaining at the beach, in the backyard, or at lakeside in the country.

Potluck is perfect for this occasion, especially since the head count has to be flexible, as those who are invited inevitably ask to bring extra last-minute house guests and children's friends.

⌒ THE MENU ⌒

Late Summer Sangria
Farm Stand Gazpacho
Greek Roasted Eggplant Salad
Mediterranean Couscous Salad
Mother's Spiked Meatloaf
Homemade Mixed Grain Bread
Summertime Blueberry Squares
Whirl-Away Chocolate Cake

Steaming lobsters at the beach is for professionals to handle and requires equipment. And you do not need recipes for corn on the

cob or platters of tomatoes, both of which can always be added to this casual menu. This is one of the few occasions when it is fine to serve on good-quality paper or bamboo plates with plastic utensils.

Pitchers or big coolers of sangria poured into plastic cups, ditto for the gazpacho, perhaps with some vodka to spike the soup for adults, will get the festivities started.

"You have to have an alternate plan for rain, someplace indoors to have the party."
—Maryanne Greenfield

Platters of blueberry squares, cake, and melon are what you need for dessert (unless you plan to bring the ingredients for s'mores by the fire). If friends want to contribute to the feast, the occasion can easily handle another bowl or two of salad and more dessert items.

All this makes for a crowd-pleasing menu that can be prepared in advance and easily transported, a few feet or a few miles, to a deck, terrace, or the beach or a picnic ground.

Soft drinks, water, and juices, lots of napkins, a big trash container, and, for sitting on the sand or the ground, sheets, big beach towels, quilts, or blankets are also necessary, as are balls, pails, and shovels for the children.

ALSO SUGGESTED: *Tailgate Deviled Eggs (page 123), Summer Bean Salad (page 111), Bobby's Crisp Chicken Cutlets (page 124), Kathleen's Wheat-Free Fudge Brownies (page 130), Mary's House Oatmeal Cookies (page 84)*

Late Summer Sangria

THIS SANGRIA HAS ALWAYS BEEN SERVED AT SUNSET ON OPENING DAY OF QUAIL-HUNTING SEASON IN ARIZONA. AT MY GRANDMOTHER'S RANCH THERE WERE TABLES ON THE LAWN THAT SHE WOULD COVER WITH HER COLLECTION OF NAVAJO BLANKETS, AND THAT'S WHERE THE PITCHERS OF SANGRIA WERE STATIONED. THE DRINKS WERE POURED INTO JELLY GLASSES AND SERVED WITH ROASTED PUMPKIN SEEDS. MY HUSBAND AND I ALSO SERVE THEM AT SUNSET AFTER KAYAKING OR CANOEING WITH FRIENDS ON THE POND.

MAKES 12 SERVINGS

4 PEACHES, PITTED AND SLICED

4 NECTARINES, PITTED AND SLICED

ZEST OF 3 LEMONS

2 TEASPOONS GROUND CINNAMON

¼ CUP SUGAR

1 CUP APRICOT BRANDY

2 BOTTLES RIOJA RED WINE, CHILLED

24 OUNCES SPARKLING WATER OR CLUB SODA, CHILLED

Place the peaches, nectarines, and lemon zest in a 3-quart pitcher. Mix the cinnamon with the sugar and add it to the fruit. Stir in the apricot brandy, then slowly stir in the wine using a wooden spoon. Refrigerate at least 4 hours or overnight.

Just before serving, pour in the sparkling water. Serve over ice in wine goblets, adding a few slices of the fruit to each glass.

If you refrigerate the sangria overnight, you can use a few cinnamon sticks in place of ground cinnamon.

Farm Stand Gazpacho

MY FRIEND KRISTIN BIDDLE SHARED THIS RECIPE WITH ME RIGHT AFTER I WAS MARRIED. IT BECAME A SUMMER FAVORITE. MY HUSBAND AND I LIKE SPICY FOODS, SO WE ADJUST THE TABASCO TO GIVE IT MORE KICK. WE ALSO LIKE IT ON THE CHUNKY SIDE, BUT YOU CAN PUREE THE INGREDIENTS IF YOU LIKE A SMOOTHER TEXTURE.

MAKES 12 SMALL SERVINGS

"Keep decorations simple; use sea shells to surround candles in hurricanes, and bags of sand to weigh down tablecloths."

—Coco Kopelman

1 CLOVE GARLIC

1 MEDIUM ONION, CHOPPED

1 SMALL GREEN BELL PEPPER, CORED, SEEDED, AND CHOPPED

2 SCALLIONS, CHOPPED

1 CUCUMBER, PEELED, SEEDED, AND CHOPPED

2 MEDIUM RIPE TOMATOES, PEELED, SEEDED, AND DICED

1 TEASPOON CHOPPED TARRAGON LEAVES

1 TEASPOON CHOPPED BASIL LEAVES

4 CUPS COLD TOMATO JUICE

JUICE OF 1 LEMON

2 TABLESPOONS RED WINE VINEGAR

DASH OF GROUND CUMIN

DASH OF TABASCO SAUCE, OR TO TASTE

1 TABLESPOON MINCED CILANTRO LEAVES

2 TABLESPOONS EXTRA VIRGIN OLIVE OIL

SALT AND FRESHLY GROUND BLACK PEPPER

Turn on a food processor and drop in the garlic clove through the feed tube. Stop the machine, place the onion, green pepper, and scallions in the bowl and pulse until very finely chopped. Add the cucumber, tomatoes, tarragon, and basil and pulse until the mixture is well combined but not perfectly smooth. Transfer the mixture to a large bowl.

Add the tomato juice, lemon juice, vinegar, cumin, and Tabasco. Cover and chill for at least 2 hours. Stir in the cilantro and oil, season with salt and pepper, and serve in small cups.

The texture of the soup should have some character but not be so thick that it's hard to sip from a cup. To make it perfectly smooth, it's best to process it in a blender and roast the green peppers by holding them over a flame until the skin blisters so it can be stripped off.

CATHERINE CAREY

Greek Roasted Eggplant Salad

⁓

THIS SALAD IS ALWAYS PART OF ANY SUMMER CELEBRATION FOR MY FAMILY.
I FIRST TASTED IT AS A CHILD WITH MY GREEK MOTHER AND GRANDMOTHER,
AND IT BRINGS BACK MEMORIES OF POOLSIDE PARTIES WITH OUR FAMILY
AND FRIENDS IN GREENWICH, CONNECTICUT. SOMETIMES I MAKE THE
SALAD WITH A CHUNKY TEXTURE, BUT IT CAN ALSO BE MADE INTO A DIP BY
PROCESSING IT FOR A FEW MINUTES UNTIL PERFECTLY SMOOTH.

MAKES 12 SERVINGS

2 EGGPLANTS, EACH ABOUT 1 POUND
2 CLOVES GARLIC, MINCED
⅓ CUP EXTRA VIRGIN OLIVE OIL
¼ CUP MINCED FLAT-LEAF PARSLEY LEAVES
SALT AND FRESHLY GROUND BLACK PEPPER
½ CUP PLAIN GREEK YOGURT, OPTIONAL
TOMATO SLICES, ONION SLICES, AND KALAMATA OLIVES FOR GARNISH
PITA CHIPS OR TOASTED PITA BREAD TRIANGLES FOR DIPPING

Preheat the oven to 350 degrees.

Pierce the eggplants with a fork, place on a foil-lined baking sheet, and
bake until soft, about 1 hour.

Dip the eggplants in cold water, slice off the tops, and peel the skin.

Turn on a food processor and drop the garlic in through the feed tube.
Stop the machine, place the eggplant flesh, oil, and parsley in the bowl
and pulse until finely chopped. Remove to a bowl and season with salt and
pepper. Fold in the yogurt, if using.

Mound the eggplant mixture on a plate and garnish with the tomatoes,
onions, and olives. Serve with a basket of pita chips or toasted pita bread
triangles for dipping.

*Instead of turning on the oven in summer the pricked eggplants can be
cooked one at a time in a microwave oven on a dish for 15 minutes each.*

CATHERINE CAREY

Mediterranean Couscous Salad

I WAS FIRST INTRODUCED TO A COLD COUSCOUS SALAD BY AN OLD FRIEND FROM HIGH SCHOOL. HIS FAMILY WAS FROM FRANCE AND HIS MOTHER ENTERTAINED ST. TROPEZ-STYLE POOLSIDE IN GREENWICH, CONNECTICUT, AND OFTEN SERVED MEDITERRANEAN DELICACIES. I ALWAYS REGRETTED NOT ASKING HER FOR THIS RECIPE SO I HAD TO CREATE MY OWN. I HAVE BEEN MAKING IT FOR YEARS AND OFTEN SPUR OF THE MOMENT WITH WHATEVER INGREDIENTS HAPPEN TO BE IN MY REFRIGERATOR. IT IS MOST DELICIOUS WHEN MADE WITH FRESH HERBS FROM THE GARDEN.

MAKES 12 SERVINGS

2 CUPS COUSCOUS
¼ CUP EXTRA VIRGIN OLIVE OIL
1 PINT GRAPE TOMATOES, HALVED
1 ENGLISH CUCUMBER, PEELED AND DICED
½ CUP CHOPPED FLAT-LEAF PARSLEY LEAVES
½ CUP CHOPPED MINT LEAVES
4 SCALLIONS, TRIMMED AND CHOPPED
JUICE OF 2 LEMONS
1½ CUPS CRUMBLED FETA CHEESE
SALT AND FRESHLY GROUND BLACK PEPPER TO TASTE

Bring 3 cups water to a boil in a saucepan. Stir in the couscous, cover, remove from the heat, and set aside for 5 minutes. Transfer the couscous to a large bowl and fold in the oil, tossing with a fork as the couscous cools to keep the grains from clumping. When the couscous has cooled, fold in the remaining ingredients. Transfer to a large serving bowl.

Couscous comes in several textures. For this recipe, medium couscous is preferable to very fine couscous.

Mother's Spiked Meatloaf

I AM SURE YOU HAVE A MILLION MEATLOAF RECIPES, BUT THIS ONE IS SO SIMPLE
I OFTEN WHIP UP A DOUBLE BATCH. HORSERADISH IS THE SECRET INGREDIENT.
THIS IS THE DISH THAT EVERYONE ASKS FOR, AND MEN LOVE IT. IT'S GREAT
MADE A DAY IN ADVANCE AND WARMED UP BEFORE SERVING.

MAKES 12 SERVINGS

1 TABLESPOON EXTRA VIRGIN OLIVE OIL
1 MEDIUM ONION, FINELY CHOPPED
2 CLOVES GARLIC, MINCED
1½ CUPS FRESH OR CANNED TOMATO PUREE
2½ POUNDS GROUND SIRLOIN
1 CUP FINE PLAIN BREAD CRUMBS
3 TABLESPOONS DIJON MUSTARD
3 TABLESPOONS PREPARED HORSERADISH
SALT AND FRESHLY GROUND BLACK PEPPER

Preheat the oven to 350 degrees.

Heat the oil in a skillet over medium heat, add the onion and garlic,
and sauté until softened and just beginning to brown. Stir in the tomato
puree, remove from the heat, and set aside.

Place the meat in a large bowl and break it up using a fork or your hands.
Add the bread crumbs, mustard, horseradish, and all but 3 tablespoons of the
seasoned tomato puree, mixing until the ingredients are thoroughly blended.
Season with salt and pepper to taste. Pack the mixture into a 9 by 5 by 3-inch
loaf pan. Spread the reserved tomato mixture on top. Place in the oven and
bake for 1½ hours. Remove from the oven and cool before slicing.

*The meatloaf can also be shaped into one or two mounds and baked free-standing in a
shallow pan instead of fitting it tightly into a loaf pan. It's best to use freshly ground beef.
Ask the butcher to grind it for you rather than buying preground beef.*

LAURA HARRIS

Homemade Mixed Grain Bread

MY MOTHER HAS MADE THIS BREAD FOR AS LONG AS I CAN REMEMBER. WHEN I VISIT HER SHE ALWAYS SENDS ME HOME WITH LOAVES OF IT OR THE DOUGH, WHICH I THEN BAKE AND TRY TO PASS OFF AS MY OWN HANDIWORK. NOBODY EVER BELIEVES ME!

MAKES 2 GENEROUS LOAVES

ABOUT 4 CUPS ALL-PURPOSE FLOUR

2 CUPS WHOLE WHEAT FLOUR

1½ TEASPOONS SALT

¼ CUP SUGAR

½ TEASPOON BAKING SODA

1½ TEASPOONS BAKING POWDER

1 STICK (¼ POUND) UNSALTED BUTTER, SLIGHTLY SOFTENED

1 PACKET ACTIVE DRY YEAST

1¾ CUPS CULTURED BUTTERMILK, AT ROOM TEMPERATURE

3 TABLESPOONS UNSALTED BUTTER, MELTED

Place the flours in a large bowl, add the salt, sugar, baking soda, and baking powder, and whisk to combine. Use your fingertips or a pastry blender to cut in the butter until the dry ingredients are somewhat mealy.

Dissolve the yeast in ½ cup warm water and set aside for a few minutes. Add the buttermilk and the yeast mixture to the dry ingredients and knead by hand to form a dough. Knead the dough in the bowl or on a work surface, adding just a little more all-purpose flour if needed, until the dough is springy and no longer sticky.

Transfer the dough to a clean bowl brushed with a little of the melted butter. Cover with plastic wrap and refrigerate for 12 to 24 hours, until doubled in size.

Remove the dough from the refrigerator, punch it down, and place it on a work surface. Divide the dough in half. Flatten each half and roll or stretch it into a rectangle 8 inches by 12 inches. From the narrower side, roll each up like a jelly roll. Brush two 8-inch loaf pans with some of the remaining melted butter. Place each roll in a pan seam side down. Brush the tops with the remaining melted butter. Set aside at room temperature until nearly doubled, 1 hour or less.

Preheat the oven to 375 degrees.

Place the breads in the oven and bake for 30 to 40 minutes, until nicely browned and the loaves shrink slightly from the edges of the pans. Remove from the oven and cool on a rack for 10 minutes, then remove the loaves from the pans and cool completely before slicing.

⊰ This bread's slow rise in the refrigerator enhances its flavor. The bread ⊱
freezes extremely well. For a delicious breakfast bread, the flattened dough
can be brushed with a little melted butter and sprinkled with cinnamon and
sugar and some raisins before it is rolled up into the pans.

"Summer entertaining is about a very informal buffet done on the backyard deck, with the bounty of summer foods: steamed lobsters, fresh corn, and deep red, fragrant tomatoes with shredded basil. Locally made ice cream and chocolate brownies for dessert will satisfy all ages."
—Coco Kopelman

"A good beach party has great music and lighting. For music, a friend who can play guitar is key. Or you can hire a steel band. But if these are not available, an iPod hooked up to a car radio or portable speaker system can do the trick just as well. For lighting, covered lanterns, torches, and bonfires set the mood. If wind is a problem, you can buy LED lights to use in the lanterns instead of candles because they will not blow out."
—Kathy Thomas

SARAH S. POWERS

Summertime Blueberry Squares

For some it's no white pants until Memorial Day, for others it's no linen past Labor Day, and in our house it was no Blueberry Squares until July 4th. We celebrated summer's arrival by making these tasty treats for our annual 4th of July fireworks picnic and enjoyed them all the way through Labor Day. My mom lined us up for many kitchen duties over the years, but prepping blueberries was always our favorite and also the easiest. So get your kids involved in the preparation of these squares and make it a family affair!

3 sticks (¾ pound) unsalted butter, chilled and diced
3⅔ cups plus 3 tablespoons all-purpose flour
2 teaspoons salt
1⅓ cups sugar
2 large eggs, separated
2 pints blueberries

Preheat the oven to 400 degrees. Use some of the butter to grease a jelly roll pan with sides, 10 by 15 inches.

Place 2⅔ cups of the flour, the salt, and 2 teaspoons of the sugar in a food processor and pulse briefly to blend. Add 2 sticks of the butter and pulse until the mixture is crumbly.

In a medium bowl, beat the egg yolks with ½ cup ice water, sprinkle over the flour mixture in the processor, and pulse until a dough starts to form. Remove the dough from the machine. Do not wash the machine. Knead the dough once or twice so it comes together, then press it into the bottom and sides of the pan. Sprinkle the dough with 3 tablespoons of the flour and refrigerate for 15 minutes.

Preheat the oven to 400 degrees.

In a medium bowl, beat the egg whites until very soft peaks form. Gradually beat in ¼ cup of the sugar until stiff peaks form. Fold in the blueberries. Spread this mixture over the dough.

Combine the remaining 1 cup flour and remaining sugar in the food processor. Add the remaining stick of butter and pulse to make crumbs. Spread over the berry mixture.

Place in the oven and bake for about 35 minutes, until the top is lightly browned and the berries are bubbling. Remove from the oven and cool, then cut into bars or squares.

❧ It pays to invest in a heavy-duty, professional-quality jelly roll pan ☙
that will not twist or warp in the oven.

Whirl-Away Chocolate Cake

THIS CAKE TRAVELS VERY WELL AND STAYS MOIST, SO IT'S GREAT FOR PICNICS.
THE RECIPE COMES FROM MY GREAT-GRANDMOTHER, WHO WAS A
WONDERFUL BAKER. IT IS A GREAT RECIPE TO MAKE WITH CHILDREN—THEY LOVE
PUTTING IN THE WHITE AND CHOCOLATE BATTERS AND SWIRLING THEM TOGETHER.

MAKES 12 SERVINGS

1½ STICKS (6 OUNCES) UNSALTED BUTTER, SOFTENED

2½ CUPS SIFTED ALL-PURPOSE FLOUR

1½ TEASPOONS BAKING POWDER

¾ TEASPOON BAKING SODA

½ TEASPOON SALT

1½ OUNCES UNSWEETENED CHOCOLATE

1⅔ CUPS SUGAR

3 LARGE EGGS

1 CUP CULTURED BUTTERMILK

1 TEASPOON VANILLA EXTRACT

Use a little of the butter to grease a loaf pan 9 by 5 by 3 inches. Dust the pan with a little of the flour. Put the remaining butter into the bowl of an electric mixer. Whisk the flour in another bowl with the baking powder, ½ teaspoon of the baking soda, and the salt.

Place the chocolate, the remaining ¼ teaspoon baking soda, 1 tablespoon of the sugar, and 2 tablespoons water in a small saucepan. Place over low heat and heat until the chocolate melts. Stir.

Preheat the oven to 325 degrees.

In a large bowl, beat the butter with the remaining sugar until light. Beat in the eggs one at a time. Stir in the flour mixture in three additions alternating with the buttermilk. Stir in the vanilla. Remove one-third of the batter to another bowl and stir the melted chocolate mixture into it.

Alternately drop generous spoonfuls of the white batter and the chocolate batter into the pan. Use a table knife to cut down through the batters in a zig-zag motion to mingle them without thoroughly mixing them. Place the pan in the oven and bake for about 1 hour and 15 minutes, until the top is lightly browned and a cake tester comes out clean. Remove from the oven, cool, then remove from the pan.

❧ There were no microwave ovens in great-grandmother's day, but now the ☙ chocolate, baking soda, sugar, and water can be combined and microwaved on high for about a minute, just until the chocolate melts. Effectively marbleizing the cake means not overdoing it—cut down into the batter and zig-zag back and forth just a few times. Less is better than more.

Supper for the Grown-ups
HALLOWEEN

Perhaps the children are tucked in bed or too old to be princesses and superheroes. And what if there are no little candy bars scattered about the house for parents to sneak while inspecting the trick-or-treat bags? What is a grown-up to do? In New York apartment buildings and brownstones, there will always be children ringing the doorbell, and there's your excuse to buy candy. Decorate the front door, or, outside the city, the porch or the yard. It's becoming more and more of a tradition for adults to dress up in costumes on Halloween, taking a cue from children who parade in costumes on the streets of New York on their way to school. Why not consider a costume party for adult friends?

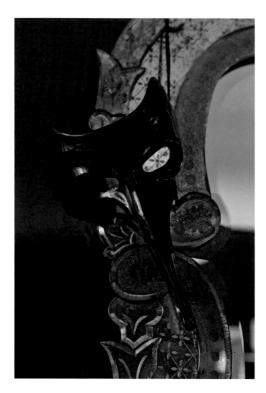

"Halloween is a favorite time of year in our home. We all share fall birthdays and as a child I had many Halloween birthday parties. We decorate our home with pumpkins, ghosts, black cats, and witches, and I always bring out my favorite witch's hat to wear while trick or treating with my boys. Once Halloween is over, everything gets packed away — except the pumpkins which are reused for the Thanksgiving holidays."

— Kelly Forsberg

"One of our neighbors outside of the city surprised us with to-go cups of red and white wine for the adults who accompany their children going trick-or-treating in the neighborhood."

— Maryanne Greenfield

"Halloween is one of my favorite holidays because we always spend it at my mother's farm in Valley Forge where I grew up. It also happens to be my brother's birthday, so it's a holiday that's filled with traditions that date back to our childhood. My mother really goes over the top with the decorations. She puts scarecrows, pumpkins, and bales of hay on our front lawn and makes the front porch look like a cemetery. For dinner we decorate the table with jack-o'-lanterns and gourds and attach black spiders to my mother's napkin rings. It's incredibly festive."

—Tory Burch

❧ THE MENU ❧

BUTTERNUT SQUASH SOUP WITH PARMESAN AND SAGE

PATSY'S POPOVERS

BEEF STROGANOFF IN A NEW YORK MINUTE

SWEET AND SOUR RED CABBAGE

MOIST AUTUMN APPLE CAKE

The combination of autumn and an evocative holiday can suggest all kinds of creative menus and table decorations. An all-black menu can start with caviar. Squid ink pasta, beluga (black) lentils, black bean soup, blackened fish or chicken breasts, black mushrooms (there's a kind called trumpet of death), black grapes with a type of cheese that comes coated with dried grape seeds, and licorice.

This menu has not been inspired by Macbeth's witches but takes the season as its cue, with a smooth butternut squash soup accompanied by popovers, then a casserole-style crowd-pleasing interpretation of beef stroganoff that is easy to prepare. It is given an earthy turn served with red cabbage alongside, and is followed by a tender apple cake. Aside from the popovers, it's a make-in-advance menu. A red wine, especially a peppery shiraz from Australia (or a syrah from California), would accompany it in style.

ALSO SUGGESTED: *Silken Mushroom Soup (page 36), Ann's Polenta with Wild Mushroom Ragoût (page 236), Prosciutto and Arugula Salad (page 55), Harvest Dinner Salad (page 176), Dad's Flemish Pork Stew (page 66), Texas Corn Pudding (page 127), Ilana's Pumpkin Muffins (page 178), Favorite Apple Pie (page 184), Besso's Feathery Pecan Puffs (page 30)*

Butternut Squash Soup with Parmesan and Sage

THIS SOUP HAS A LONG HISTORY—I CONCOCTED IT AS A NEWLYWED WHEN MOST OF THE BUTTERNUT SQUASH SOUP RECIPES I TRIED WERE TOO SWEET. I BEGAN SERVING IT FROM ITALIAN COFFEE MUGS AT RELAXED FALL SUPPERS AND EVENTUALLY IT BECAME PART OF OUR THANKSGIVING DINNERS.

MAKES 6 TO 8 SERVINGS

1 BUTTERNUT SQUASH, PEELED, CUT IN HALF, SEEDED, AND CUBED

2 LEEKS, WHITE PART ONLY, CLEANED AND CHOPPED

2 CARROTS, SLICED

½ CUP CHOPPED ONION

2 TABLESPOONS UNSALTED BUTTER

1 TEASPOON SALT

4 CUPS WELL-SEASONED CHICKEN STOCK

2 CUPS FRESHLY GRATED PARMIGIANO-REGGIANO

½ CUP HEAVY CREAM, OPTIONAL

SAGE LEAVES FOR GARNISH

EXTRA VIRGIN OLIVE OIL FOR DRIZZLING, OPTIONAL

Place the squash, leeks, carrots, and onion in a saucepan. Add the butter and salt, cover, and cook over low heat until the vegetables start to soften, 10 to 15 minutes. Add the chicken stock, bring to a simmer, and cook, covered, until the vegetables are soft, about 30 minutes.

Meanwhile, preheat the oven to 350 degrees.

Using a tablespoon, drop about 24 small mounds of the cheese onto a nonstick baking sheet. Place in the oven and bake until the cheese melts and forms lacy crisps. Remove from the oven and cool. Set aside.

When the vegetables are soft, cool briefly, then puree them, along with the stock, in a blender or food processor in two batches. Return the puree to the saucepan and bring to a simmer. Season with salt to taste. Add the heavy cream, if using, and heat through. Serve in bowls or mugs, each garnished with Parmesan crisps and a sage leaf. If you like, drizzle the surface of the soup with olive oil.

❦ These cheese crisps are what Italians from the Friuli region in the northeastern ❦ part of the country call frico. *Even without the soup they are wonderful to serve as cocktail nibbles, alongside a salad or to garnish a plate of risotto.*

Patsy's Popovers

This recipe can make any meal festive. It came from Patsy Hansen, one of my mother's dearest friends—Patsy would bring the popovers to our house and my mother would serve them with roast beef. And they smell absolutely delicious while they bake!

Makes 12

10 tablespoons (1¼ sticks) unsalted butter, melted and cooled
6 large eggs
1 teaspoon salt
2 cups whole milk
2 cups all-purpose flour, sifted

Preheat the oven to 375 degrees and brush 12 popover molds or a large 12-cup muffin tin with 4 tablespoons of the butter.

Place the eggs in an electric mixer, blender, or food processor and beat until light and bubbly. Add the salt, the remaining 6 tablespoons melted butter, the milk, and flour and process until well blended. Divide the batter among the buttered tins.

Place in the oven and bake for about 45 minutes, until puffed and golden brown. Remove from the molds and serve immediately.

The popover batter is similar to Yorkshire pudding, which is baked in beef drippings in a pan alongside the roast beef. It also makes the puffed "Dutch baby" pancake that can be a breakfast or dessert treat. Popovers can even be used like savory cream puffs, baked, split, and filled with creamed seafood or chicken or even with the quick beef stroganoff from this menu minus the noodles.

"For guests who don't like coming in costume, have a tray of masks, hats, feather boas, and the like that they can put on as they walk in. You can decorate the table with creepy things and create an all-black menu."
—Coco Kopelman

Beef Stroganoff in a New York Minute

THIS IS A FAVORITE OF MY BROTHER DAVID, WHO WAS A PILOT IN THE MARINES. MY MOTHER MADE IT FOR HIM WHEN HE RETURNED FROM IRAQ IN THE MIDDLE OF SUMMER, EVEN THOUGH IT IS NOT A LIGHT SUMMER DISH. IT'S A DELICIOUS SUPPER DISH THAT'S EASY TO MAKE AND CAN SERVE A CROWD AROUND HOLIDAY TIME.

MAKES 6 SERVINGS

2 TABLESPOONS EXTRA VIRGIN OLIVE OIL

1 LARGE ONION, THINLY SLICED

6 OUNCES WHITE MUSHROOMS, THINLY SLICED

1 POUND GROUND SIRLOIN

2 TABLESPOONS UNSALTED BUTTER

2 TABLESPOONS ALL-PURPOSE FLOUR

1½ CUPS HOT BEEF STOCK

SALT AND FRESHLY GROUND BLACK PEPPER

2 TEASPOONS DIJON MUSTARD

1 POUND NOODLES OR FETTUCCINE

6 TABLESPOONS SOUR CREAM

1 TABLESPOON MINCED FRESH DILL

Heat the oil in a skillet over medium heat. Add the onion and mushrooms and sauté until they barely start to brown. Add the meat and cook, breaking it up with a fork, until it has lost its pink color and is evenly crumbly. Remove from the heat.

Melt the butter in a medium saucepan over medium heat. Whisk in the flour, cook a minute or so, then gradually whisk in the stock to make a creamy sauce. Season with salt and pepper and whisk in the mustard. Pour the sauce over the meat and mushroom mixture. Reheat briefly and check the seasoning again. Set aside.

Bring a large pot of salted water to a boil for the pasta. Cook the noodles or fettuccine according to the package directions and drain well. Place in a large warm bowl. Reheat the meat mixture and fold in the sour cream. Spoon the meat over the noodles, garnish with the dill, and serve.

⸙ The difference between this recipe and traditional beef stroganoff is ⸙
that the latter is made with sliced beef, the tenderloin or sirloin.
Making it with ground beef is not only gentler on the wallet, it is homier
and simpler to prepare and overcooking is never an issue.

Sweet and Sour Red Cabbage

THIS IS A SIDE DISH THAT MY MOTHER, WHO IS SWEDISH, ALWAYS SERVED WITH TURKEY DINNER FOR THANKSGIVING, BUT IT WORKS AT OTHER TIMES AS WELL. IT'S A BIT TART, SO IT SUITS A BIG MEAL, SINCE TARTNESS WHETS THE APPETITE.

MAKES 6 SERVINGS

6 THICK SLICES COUNTRY BACON, DICED
1 LARGE ONION, CHOPPED
1 MEDIUM HEAD RED CABBAGE, CORED AND SHREDDED
1 CUP UNSWEETENED APPLESAUCE
3 TABLESPOONS LIGHT BROWN SUGAR
¼ CUP RED WINE VINEGAR, OR MORE TO TASTE
SALT TO TASTE
1 TABLESPOON CARAWAY SEEDS

Place the bacon in a heavy 4-quart saucepan over medium heat and cook until lightly browned. Add the onion and continue cooking until golden. Reduce the heat to low and start adding the cabbage a little at a time, adding more as it wilts down.

Stir in the remaining ingredients. Cover and simmer for about 45 minutes, until the cabbage is very tender. Taste and add more salt and vinegar if needed. Serve immediately, or set aside and reheat before serving.

The balance of sweet and sour can be adjusted to suit your taste, but it's always a good idea to cook red cabbage with some vinegar or other acid— the applesauce might be enough. Otherwise it might take on a bluish cast (a reaction to the presence of an alkaline compound in the cabbage)—which could be a little too creepy, even for Halloween.

MARIA VILLALBA

Moist Autumn Apple Cake

HERE IS A DESSERT MY FAMILY WOULD SERVE FOR THANKSGIVING, BUT IT'S PERFECT ANYTIME IN THE FALL. A SCOOP OF VANILLA ICE CREAM ON THE SIDE IS A DELICIOUS ACCOMPANIMENT.

½ tablespoon unsalted butter, softened

3 cups all-purpose flour

1 teaspoon ground cinnamon

1 teaspoon baking soda

½ teaspoon salt

1½ cups corn oil or grapeseed oil

¾ cup granulated sugar

½ cup light brown sugar

3 large eggs

1 teaspoon vanilla extract

3 Granny Smith or Golden Delicious apples,
peeled, cored, and sliced (about 3 cups)

1 cup raisins

2 teaspoons confectioners' sugar

Whipped cream, crème fraîche, or vanilla ice cream for serving

Preheat the oven to 350 degrees. Butter a 9-inch springform cake pan and dust it with a little of the flour.

Sift the remaining flour into a large bowl with the cinnamon, baking soda, and salt.

Place the oil in the bowl of an electric mixer. Add the granulated and brown sugars and beat for about 4 minutes, until the mixture is very creamy. Beat in the eggs one at a time, then beat in the vanilla. Gently stir the flour mixture into the oil and sugar mixture. Fold in the apples and raisins. Pour the batter into the pan and bake for about 1 hour, until golden and the top of the cake is firm to the touch. Remove from the oven and cool, then remove the sides of the pan and set aside until ready to serve. Sift confectioners' sugar over the top and serve with whipped cream, crème fraîche, or vanilla ice cream if you like.

Pears or plums can be used in place of the apples or in combination with them. Dried cranberries would be another nice addition. This is practically a casserole cake, so it can also be made in a ceramic ovenproof dish that is attractive enough to go to the table and scooped warm, right from the dish.

A True Potluck Tradition
THANKSGIVING

Without question Thanksgiving is the ultimate family occasion and an ideal time to welcome others to the table. Traditions remain strong. Those who try to vary the menu— what, no marshmallows on the sweet potatoes?—usually find themselves returning to the classics.

Decorations are simply achieved. An abundance of food, including the turkey that is always the pièce de résistance, means there has to be lots of space left at the table. The season, with its glowing orange and bronze palette, takes command. Gourds, squashes, pumpkins, leaves, and chrysanthemums provide easy and earthy decor. Miniature wrapped chocolate turkeys and festive candles are all it takes to complete the look.

THE MENU

 EBBA'S SWEDISH APPLE CIDER PUNCH

HARVEST DINNER SALAD

ILANA'S PUMPKIN MUFFINS

THE TURKEY (AS YOU LIKE IT)

CORNBREAD-PECAN STUFFING WITH DRIED FRUIT

GREEN BEANS THAT COOKED "ALL NIGHT"

FAVORITE APPLE PIE

PRALINE PUMPKIN PIE

Thanksgiving is an occasion for potluck. Everyone who comes wants to bring something. And like members of the Massachusetts Bay colony in the seventeenth century, such contributions have to be accepted. Wine, a side dish, and pie are the easiest to suggest, especially for those who are living in the city.

"For years we went to a large family feast in the country during the day and then came back to the city to do it all over again at home for friends who found themselves here without much to do. There might be visitors from abroad with no concept of Thanksgiving or those stranded here for work, or with mixed-up travel plans. They would always make it a true celebration of Thanksgiving."
—Leslie Perkin

ALSO SUGGESTED: *Butternut Squash Soup with Parmesan and Sage (page 160), Cornmeal Batter Cakes (page 64), Patsy's Popovers (page 163), Moist Autumn Apple Cake (page 168)*

"As for the Burke family's favorite celebration, Thanksgiving wins with no contest! We have a wonderful two-hundred-year-old farmhouse where four generations of our family gather, rain or shine. Behind the barn we split wood for the fireplace. Brussels sprouts are carved off their stalks on the porch. And then everyone takes turns in the kitchen chopping, pureeing, and preparing the feast. We begin dinner by singing 'We Gather Together' followed by American caviar and crème fraîche on corn blinis. Then comes the main event, turkey with all the trimmings."

—Susan Burke

Ebba's Swedish Apple Cider Punch

THIS PUNCH IS OFTEN SERVED AFTER A DAY OF HUNTING IN SWEDEN, WHERE THEY LOVE WARM DRINKS. THE RECIPE IS FROM A LONGTIME FAMILY FRIEND, COUNTESS EBBA VON ECKERMAN, WHO HAD A GREAT HUNTING LODGE. I SUBSTITUTE CRANBERRY JUICE FOR THE LINGONBERRY JUICE THEY USE IN SWEDEN AND THE TASTE IS EQUALLY DELICIOUS.

MAKES 12 SERVINGS

6 CUPS FRESH NONALCOHOLIC APPLE CIDER

2 CUPS CRANBERRY JUICE

½ CUP DARK BROWN SUGAR

12 WHOLE CLOVES

2 CINNAMON STICKS

½ TEASPOON GRATED NUTMEG

½ TEASPOON GROUND GINGER

2 ORANGES, THINLY SLICED

1 LEMON, THINLY SLICED

Combine all the ingredients except the oranges and lemon in a large pot over medium heat. Bring to a simmer and cook until the sugar dissolves. Strain, add the oranges and lemon, and serve warm.

Though this recipe is nonalcoholic, it can be made with hard cider instead, and even be spiked with applejack, Calvados, or vodka. When using unpeeled citrus fruits in a recipe—even just the zest—be sure to wash the fruit first.

"One of our family traditions is to have each guest state what he or she is thankful for, and with the wide range of ages, from five to eighty-nine, it's interesting to see the variety of themes that come up."
—Coco Kopelman

Harvest Dinner Salad

〜❦〜

WE HAVE A LOT OF BIG FAMILY DINNERS FOR HOLIDAYS, AND THIS EASY
VARIATION ON A TYPICAL GREEN SALAD COMES IN VERY HANDY AND CAN
BE MADE IN LARGE QUANTITIES. ALWAYS WAIT UNTIL THE LAST MINUTE
BEFORE TOSSING THE GREENS WITH THE DRESSING.

MAKES 8 TO 10 SERVINGS

3 CUPS DICED PEELED BUTTERNUT SQUASH

SALT

½ CUP CHOPPED TOASTED HAZELNUTS

¼ CUP EXTRA VIRGIN OLIVE OIL

¼ CUP HAZELNUT OIL

3 TABLESPOONS WHITE WINE VINEGAR

2 TEASPOONS DIJON MUSTARD

½ CUP GRATED PARMIGIANO-REGGIANO

8 CUPS MIXED SALAD GREENS SUCH AS
BABY SPINACH, ARUGULA, AND BOSTON LETTUCE

Bring a pot of salted water to a boil, add the squash, cook for 2 minutes,
or until tender, then drain and place it in a salad bowl. Add the hazelnuts.
    In a medium bowl, whisk the oils, vinegar, and mustard together.
Pour over the squash and nuts and set aside until shortly before serving.
Just before serving, add the cheese and toss. Add the greens, toss again,
and serve.

❦ *Hazelnut oil, like all nut oils, is very perishable and should be kept in the* ❦
refrigerator. You could also use sharp aged cheddar in the salad instead of
Parmigiano-Reggiano.

"My husband carves the turkey at the table. He insists on it, and he does it well."
—Nicole Limbocker

Ilana's Pumpkin Muffins

LIKE MANY OF THE CHILDREN OF DOCTORS AND OTHER STAFF IN THE PEDIATRICS DEPARTMENT AT MSKCC, MY DAUGHTER ILANA HAS SPENT MANY HOURS AS A VOLUNTEER WITH OUR PATIENTS. ILANA'S FAVORITE ACTIVITY IS BAKING WITH THE KIDS IN THE PEDIATRICS PAVILION. THE CHILDREN ESPECIALLY LOVE HER PUMPKIN MUFFINS—SO MUCH SO THAT MANY OF THEIR FAMILIES HAVE TAKEN THE RECIPE HOME WITH THEM TO PLACES ALL OVER AMERICA AND ABROAD. IN OUR FAMILY THE MUFFINS ARE NOW A THANKSGIVING TRADITION, AND FAMILY AND FRIENDS ALWAYS LEAVE WITH A BAG FULL. THEY STAY FRESH FOR DAYS, AND MAKE THE BEST COMFORT FOOD ALL YEAR-ROUND FOR CHILDREN AND ADULTS ALIKE.

"I love to spray paint pumpkins in gold, bronze, and silver to give them a warm and dazzling effect. It's also nice to mix in exotic white pumpkins as an accent."

— Chesie Breen

MAKES 12 MUFFINS

1⅓ CUPS GRANULATED SUGAR

¼ CUP LIGHT BROWN SUGAR

2 LARGE EGGS

½ CUP VEGETABLE OIL

1⅔ CUPS ALL-PURPOSE FLOUR

1 TEASPOON BAKING SODA

¾ TEASPOON SALT

½ TEASPOON GROUND CINNAMON

½ TEASPOON GRATED NUTMEG

1 CUP UNSEASONED PUMPKIN OR SQUASH PUREE, FRESH, CANNED, OR FROZEN

2 TABLESPOONS SHELLED PUMPKIN SEEDS (PEPITAS)

Preheat the oven to 350 degrees and line a 12-cup 2½-inch muffin tin with fluted paper liners.

In a large bowl, combine the sugars, eggs, oil, and ⅓ cup water. In a medium bowl, whisk together the flour, baking soda, salt, cinnamon, and nutmeg. Add the dry ingredients to the wet ingredients and stir well. Fold in the pumpkin puree. Spoon the batter into the muffin cups and sprinkle the pumpkin seeds on top.

Place in the oven and bake for 20 to 25 minutes, until the tops spring back when lightly touched.

Sylvie Bigar, who tested some of the recipes for this book, baked these muffins with her children. Sébastien, who is six, loved them, and Sylvie said they reminded her of French spice bread, pain d'épices. Because they do not require an electric mixer, they are a perfect recipe to make with small children, who can help measure, then stir the ingredients and fill the muffin tins. The muffins can also be baked in 1½-inch mini-muffin tins to yield about 3 dozen (reducing the baking time to about 15 minutes) for a lovely little nibble to serve alongside the Thanksgiving salad.

ASHLEY POTTER

Cornbread–Pecan Stuffing with Dried Fruit

THIS IS MY MOTHER'S RECIPE, A FAIRLY RECENT ONE. INSTEAD OF MAKING JUST ONE KIND OF STUFFING, TO ROAST INSIDE THE TURKEY, SHE STARTED PREPARING TWO, ONE TO STUFF THE BIRD AND THE OTHER TO BAKE IN A CASSEROLE AS AN ALTERNATE SIDE DISH. WE ALL LOVE HER TRADITIONAL STUFFING, AND THIS IS A VARIATION MADE BY ADDING CORNBREAD, DRIED FRUIT, AND PECANS, WHICH ARE GREAT FOR THANKSGIVING DINNER.

3 STICKS (¾ POUND) UNSALTED BUTTER

1½ CUPS FINELY CHOPPED CELERY

1½ CUPS FINELY CHOPPED ONION

1½ TEASPOONS DRIED SAGE

1½ CUPS PECANS, TOASTED AND CHOPPED

¼ CUP DRIED APRICOTS, QUARTERED

⅓ CUP GOLDEN RAISINS

⅔ CUP CHOPPED PARSLEY

3 CUPS CUBED STALE COUNTRY BREAD OR UNSEASONED CROUTONS

3 CUPS CUBED STALE CORNBREAD OR UNSEASONED CROUTONS

SALT AND FRESHLY GROUND BLACK PEPPER

ABOUT 1½ CUPS WELL-FLAVORED CHICKEN OR TURKEY STOCK

Melt half of the butter in a very large skillet over medium heat. Add the celery and onion and sauté until softened but not browned. Stir in the sage.

Place the pecans, apricots, raisins, and parsley in a large bowl. Mix in the onion and celery. Add the bread cubes, season with salt and pepper, and mix well.

Melt the remaining butter in the skillet. Add the mixture from the bowl and sauté, adding stock to moisten the ingredients so they are damp but not soggy, until everything is well combined.

Cool and either refrigerate the stuffing until the turkey is ready to be stuffed or transfer the stuffing to a buttered 10- to 12-cup casserole and bake it at 350 degrees for 40 minutes, then serve.

Sautéing the stuffing mixture as you add the stock makes all the difference. It adds a measure of crispness to the mixture, helping to keep it from becoming soggy. These days you can buy prepared croutons—unseasoned are best, but if your oven has a pilot light, you can put slices of bread in the turned-off oven overnight and you will have stale bread for your stuffing on Thanksgiving morning. Plan further ahead and your bread can be left out to dry on your kitchen counter for a couple of days. Sautéed mushrooms and even crumbled sausage can easily be added to this recipe.

Green Beans That Cooked "All Night"

This dish has been in our family forever. My sister Katherine has taken over this recipe, and she is hence in charge of the beans. One year she could not join us for the holiday and my husband was disappointed. "That's too bad," he said, "but what about the green beans?"

MAKES 8 SERVINGS

2 OUNCES SMOKY BACON, DICED
1 MEDIUM ONION, DICED
2 POUNDS GREEN BEANS, TRIMMED
6 TABLESPOONS WHITE WINE VINEGAR
SALT AND FRESHLY GROUND BLACK PEPPER

Preheat the oven to 200 degrees.

Place the bacon in a 3-quart saucepan over medium heat. Add the onion and cook until the bacon and onion are lightly browned. Stir in the beans, vinegar, and 1 cup water and bring to a simmer. Season to taste with salt and pepper.

Transfer to a baking dish, place in the oven, and bake, uncovered, for at least 2 hours, basting from time to time, until the beans are very tender. Serve immediately or remove from the oven and reheat just before serving.

There is a time and place for undercooked vegetables—and an argument for well-cooked ones. Beans that are crisp may be fine on a platter of crudités, but there is something to be said for green beans that are succulently tender and flavorful, even if their color is less appealing. These beans, which can cook overnight, assuming you trust your unattended appliances, do not necessarily require quite that much time, as there is not much improvement after a couple of hours. The nice part is that the beans can be served just warm (reheated in the microwave instead of commanding precious oven real estate at Thanksgiving) and even at room temperature.

Favorite Apple Pie

⌇⌇⌇

THIS IS THE EASIEST APPLE PIE TO MAKE. BAKE IT IN A PRETTY PIE
DISH, SERVE IT WARM, AND DON'T SKIMP ON THE MELTED BUTTER
POURED OVER THE UNBAKED FILLING.

MAKES 8 TO 10 SERVINGS

PASTRY FOR TWO-CRUST PIE (RECIPE FOLLOWS)
½ CUP SUGAR
½ TEASPOON GROUND CINNAMON
1 CUP GRAHAM CRACKER CRUMBS
6 TART APPLES (GRANNY SMITH, CORTLAND, MUTSU, FUJI),
PEELED, CORED, AND SLICED ½ INCH THICK
PINCH OF SALT
4 TO 6 TABLESPOONS UNSALTED BUTTER, MELTED
1 EGG YOLK BEATEN WITH 1 TABLESPOON WATER

Divide the pastry in half but not quite equally. Roll out the larger half to
a 13-inch circle and line a 9-inch glass pie plate, leaving an overhang.
Trim the overhang evenly to 1 inch beyond the rim.

Mix the sugar and cinnamon together in a large bowl. Add half the
graham cracker crumbs and fold in the apples. Pile the mixture into the pie
plate. Sprinkle with the remaining graham cracker crumbs. Drizzle on the
melted butter, using more or less to taste.

Preheat the oven to 350 degrees.

Roll out the remaining pastry and place over the apples. Use kitchen
scissors to trim the edge of the top pastry to meet the edge of the pie plate.
Fold the overhanging dough from the bottom crust over the edge of the top
crust and crimp with your fingertips or press with the tines of a fork. Brush
the pastry with the egg yolk mixture. Cut a few decorative slits in the top.

Bake the pie for about 1 hour, until browned. Remove from the oven
and serve warm, cooled, or reheated.

❧ Adding graham cracker crumbs to an apple pie filling is not only unusual, ❧ it is ingenious. It thickens the juices without flour and also adds a deliciously nutty flavor. Consider the crumb trick for other fruit pies, blueberry, for example, or peach. You could also try using gingersnap crumbs.

FLORENCE FABRICANT

PASTRY FOR PIES

AFTER MANY, MANY YEARS OF TRYING AND TESTING VARIOUS RECIPES
AND TECHNIQUE FOR PIE PASTRY, I HAVE NOW DECIDED THAT THIS ONE GIVES
THE VERY BEST RESULTS AND IS EASY TO ROLL.

MAKES PASTRY FOR A TWO-CRUST 9-INCH PIE
(USE HALF THE RECIPE FOR A SINGLE-CRUST PIE)

2½ CUPS ALL-PURPOSE FLOUR, PLUS MORE FOR ROLLING
1 TEASPOON SALT
2 TABLESPOONS SUGAR
12 TABLESPOONS (1½ STICKS) COLD UNSALTED BUTTER, DICED
2 LARGE EGG YOLKS

Place the flour, salt, and sugar in a food processor and pulse to blend. Add the butter and pulse until the mixture is crumbly. Beat the egg yolks with 5 tablespoons cold water. Open the machine and sprinkle in the egg yolk mixture. Pulse quickly about 15 times. If the ingredients do not start to come together to form a dough, add another tablespoon or so of the water and pulse again. Do not process the dough until it forms a ball in the machine, but it should hold together when you pick some up with your fingers.

Lightly dust a work surface with flour. Dump out the contents of the food processor and quickly smooth it into a flat disk. Wrap in plastic and refrigerate for at least 30 minutes.

Praline Pumpkin Pie

I CANNOT REMEMBER WHERE I FOUND THIS RECIPE—ALL I KNOW IS
THAT I ALWAYS SERVE IT FOR THANKSGIVING, AND EVEN PEOPLE WHO
THINK THEY DO NOT LIKE PUMPKIN PIE LOVE THIS ONE.

MAKES 8 TO 10 SERVINGS

½ RECIPE PASTRY FOR PIES (PAGE 185)

2 TABLESPOONS APRICOT JAM

1 CUP PLUS 2 TABLESPOONS CANNED, FROZEN,
OR FRESHLY COOKED UNSEASONED PUMPKIN PUREE

¾ CUP GRANULATED SUGAR

1 ¾ CUPS HEAVY CREAM

6 TABLESPOONS WHOLE MILK

2 LARGE EGGS, LIGHTLY BEATEN

2 TABLESPOONS DARK RUM

¾ TEASPOON GROUND CINNAMON

¾ TEASPOON GROUND GINGER

¼ TEASPOON GRATED NUTMEG

¼ TEASPOON GROUND CLOVES

½ TEASPOON SALT

½ CUP LIGHT BROWN SUGAR

½ CUP COARSELY CHOPPED PECANS

2 TABLESPOONS UNSALTED BUTTER, MELTED

Preheat the oven to 425 degrees.

Roll out the pastry and line a 9-inch glass pie pan. Trim the edges
and crimp with a fork. Line the pastry with a sheet of foil and pile in pastry
weights or dried beans. Bake the crust for 10 minutes, then remove the foil
liner and weights and bake for another 10 minutes, until lightly colored.
Remove from the oven and cool. Reduce the oven temperature to 375
degrees. Brush the bottom of the crust with the jam.

Place the pumpkin puree in a large bowl and beat in the granulated sugar, ¾ cup of the cream, the milk, eggs, rum, spices, and salt. Pour into the prepared crust, place in the oven, and bake for 20 minutes, then reduce the oven temperature to 325 degrees and bake for about 20 minutes longer, until the filling is set. Remove from the oven and cool completely on a rack.

Preheat the broiler. Combine the brown sugar, pecans, and melted butter in a small bowl and sprinkle over the top of the pie. Cover the crimped pastry edge with a strip of foil and broil for a few minutes, just until the topping bubbles, watching carefully so it does not burn. Transfer the pie to a rack and cool completely, about 1 hour.

Whip the remaining 1 cup cream and serve it with the pie.

"A cornucopia filled with miniature gourds and pumpkins always spills down the center of the table. The crisp white linen cloth and napkins are bordered with turquoise scallops. We would never let my mother change even one detail! The family flies to Chicago and knows the stuffing will always be made according to the family recipe. Sometimes having everything just as you expected is life's best treat!"
— Jamee Gregory

After the Tree Lighting
HOLIDAY COCKTAIL PARTY

There is no shortage of occasions for hosting a cocktail party in
New York. Among the most dazzling is the fall Preview Party for the
International Fine Art and Antique Dealers Show at the Park Avenue
Armory, which has benefited The Society of Memorial Sloan-Kettering
Cancer Center since the inaugural event in 1989. Patrons are invited
for a sneak preview of the show and a cocktail reception.

The members of The Society also turn out for the Park Avenue Tree
Lighting on the first Sunday in December. This tradition began in
1945 as a memorial to those who gave their lives in our nation's wars.
It continues today thanks to contributions made to The Fund for Park
Avenue. In the early evening, outside Brick Church, at Park Avenue
and 91st Street, hundreds of people—adults and children—gather
and sing Christmas carols. When it is time to light the trees, the
church minister says, "Let there be light!" Then the whole crowd
sends up a big cheer. People from all over the city join in celebrating
the beginning of the holiday season. Before and afterward there are
cocktail parties in private homes up and down the avenue.

~ THE MENU ~

ANNIE'S EGGNOG

TOASTED CHEESE PUFFS

WARM MUSHROOM ROLLS

WATER CHESTNUT–BACON SKEWERS

MINI BAKED CRAB CAKES

DOUBLE SALMON MOUSSE

SUSAN'S PORK AND CLEMENTINE BITES

ROARING TWENTIES COFFEE BAVARIAN CREAM

THE BEST BISCOTTI

A cocktail party can be as simple or as complicated as you wish: a full bar or just beer and wine; little finger sandwiches or more elaborate hors d'oeuvres; waiters or simply platters on a table. It all depends on your personal style and budget. But no matter how it is organized, there should be plenty for guests to eat and drink comfortably. Bowls of nuts and pitted olives are always good for nibbling.

This menu suggests cocktail party food to prepare in advance with some last-minute heating for some dishes, as well as more substantial fare for a buffet table and small plates. But do not skimp on the drinks, figuring one glass per person every half hour. Plan on refilling the ice bucket often during the typical two-hour span of a cocktail party. You can't have too many cocktail napkins. And don't forget to make provisions for used plates and glasses and discarded napkins.

As for the bar, glassware, not plastic, should be used, especially since this is an indoor holiday-season party, not a casual backyard summertime affair. Rented glassware has the convenience of only requiring rinsing, not washing and drying.

And in areas where the weather will be cold or inclement, consider coats and umbrellas. Instead of having people dump them on a bed, clear a closet of your coats and put them on the bed, so guests can use the closet. Closet space is a luxury, especially in New York, so if you don't have enough space, arrange for a coat rack.

"My dear friend Nancy grew up in the neighborhood of Brick Church, and the Park Avenue tree lighting is her favorite night of the year! The night before her wedding, the wedding party and all of their guests were invited to her childhood home for an early dinner that the bride made all by herself as she always does, and then everyone bundled up and went to Park Avenue to sing carols together and light the holiday trees. It's a night that my family and I will never forget."
– Heather Leeds

ALSO SUGGESTED: *Smoked Salmon Canapés (page 234),*
Quick Asparagus Hors D'Oeuvres (page 48), Tailgate Deviled Eggs (page 123),
Hungarian Walnut Kifli (page 226)

Annie's Eggnog

⁓

THIS IS A HOLIDAY-SEASON FAVORITE IN OUR FAMILY THAT
WAS CREATED BY ANNIE, WHO WORKED FOR MY MOTHER.

MAKES 3 QUARTS, ABOUT 24 SERVINGS

6 LARGE EGGS, SEPARATED

1 CUP SUGAR

2 CUPS WHOLE MILK

½ CUP RUM

½ CUP BRANDY

2 CUPS BOURBON

4 CUPS HEAVY CREAM

GRATED NUTMEG

Place the egg yolks in a heavy saucepan and whisk in the sugar. Place over low heat or in the top of a double boiler. Add the milk and cook, stirring, until the mixture thickens, just begins to give off steam, and makes a custard. Do not overcook or the eggs will curdle. Whisk in the rum, brandy, bourbon, and 2 cups of the cream. Remove from the heat and refrigerate until cold.

Just before serving, whip the egg whites until soft peaks form. Whip the remaining 2 cups cream until soft peaks form. Fold the egg whites and cream into the chilled base mixture, pour into a punch bowl, whisk again, dust with nutmeg, and serve, stirring as you ladle it into punch cups.

The original of this outrageously sumptuous recipe was made with raw eggs. These days some people are concerned about their safety, though organic eggs are less risky than plain supermarket ones. Using the yolks to make a cooked custard base for the eggnog is one way around the problem. Another is to use pasteurized whites, which are now available in supermarkets, in place of the raw whites, or even to skip the beaten egg whites entirely. A little of this eggnog goes a very long way because it is so rich.

Toasted Cheese Puffs

IN OUR LARGE FAMILY THERE WAS ALWAYS A LOT OF COOKING IN MY MOTHER'S KITCHEN. AS WE SEVEN SIBLINGS WENT OFF ON OUR OWN OR GOT MARRIED OUR COOKING BECAME A LITTLE MORE ADVENTURESOME THAN THE MEAT AND POTATOES MY MOTHER MADE. THIS HORS D'OEUVRE IS ONE THAT I OFTEN SERVE FOR FAMILY GATHERINGS AND PARTIES FOR FRIENDS.

MAKES 36

¾ CUP FRESHLY GRATED PARMIGIANO-REGGIANO
¾ CUP MAYONNAISE
1 TABLESPOON FINELY GRATED ONION
SALT AND FRESHLY GROUND BLACK PEPPER
2 LARGE EGG WHITES
36 SMALL ROUNDS BAGUETTE OR BREAD, LIGHTLY TOASTED

Preheat a broiler and line a baking sheet with foil.

In a medium bowl, mix the cheese, mayonnaise, and onion together. Season with salt and pepper.

In a separate bowl, beat the egg whites until they hold peaks. Fold into the cheese mixture.

Spoon the mixture on the toast, arrange on the baking sheet, and broil until the canapés are puffed and lightly browned.

The whipped egg whites in this recipe make these puffs lighter and more elegant than the usual cheese canapé.

"Always be gracious, no matter what may happen—be it red wine spilled all over your antique linens, a crying child, or an inebriated guest. A gracious hostess will be unflappable and serve as a distraction for any calamity that may occur."

—Muffie Potter Aston

Warm Mushroom Rolls

My mother-in-law had a reputation as a fine cook—and for good reason, as I discovered the first time I tasted these mushroom rolls, her signature hors d'oeuvre. They always vanished as soon as they came out of the oven, and they still do.

Makes 60 rolls

1 medium onion, chopped
1 shallot, chopped
3 tablespoons chopped flat-leaf parsley leaves
12 ounces white mushrooms
7 tablespoons unsalted butter
1½ tablespoons heavy cream
2 teaspoons Worcestershire sauce
Salt and freshly ground black pepper
1-pound loaf firm sandwich bread (about 15 slices)

Place the onion, shallot, and parsley in a food processor and pulse until finely minced. Remove from the processor, place the mushrooms in the food processor, and pulse until finely chopped.

Melt 2 tablespoons of the butter in a large skillet over medium heat, add the mushrooms, and sauté until lightly browned and no liquid remains in the pan. Transfer to a bowl. Add 1 tablespoon of the butter to the pan, then add the onion mixture and sauté until it starts to color. Add to the mushrooms in the bowl and mix with the cream and Worcestershire sauce. Season with salt and pepper.

Preheat the oven to 375 degrees.

Remove the crusts from the bread. Use a rolling pin to roll each slice flat. Place a heaping tablespoon of the mushroom filling over one side of the bread, then tightly roll up the bread with the filling. Melt the remaining butter. Use some of the butter to brush a foil-lined baking sheet. Place the rolls seam-side down on the baking sheet. Use the remaining butter to brush on the mushroom rolls. Place in the oven and bake for about 25 minutes, until the bread is lightly toasted. Use a serrated knife to cut each roll in 4 pieces, arrange on a platter, and serve. The finished hors d'oeuvres can be made in advance and reheated for about 10 minutes at 325 degrees.

Using white bread rolled flat as a stand-in for pastry is a venerable trick. These little tidbits are guaranteed to disappear in a flash, and they freeze extremely well.

"If ever there is a perfect time for a potluck dinner on Park Avenue, it is following the tree lighting when neighbors gather in private homes for hot cider, hot chocolate, a warm meal, and lots of holiday cookies for the children."

—Chesie Breen

Water Chestnut–Bacon Skewers

Growing up, my six sisters and I were all taught to be hostesses, and so there were always lots of cooks in the kitchen. The first time we served these hors d'oeuvres was for an engagement party for one of my sisters many years ago. In those days, there was very little catering. We prepared everything for all of our parties. We all still make them in our own houses today.

MAKES ABOUT 30

2 (8-OUNCE) CANS WATER CHESTNUTS (ABOUT 30 PIECES), DRAINED
⅓ CUP SOY SAUCE
⅔ CUP LIGHT BROWN SUGAR
8 STRIPS THICK BACON, EACH CUT INTO 4 PIECES

Rinse the water chestnuts, place them in a bowl, add the soy sauce, and set aside to marinate for a few hours, turning them from time to time.

Preheat the oven to 350 degrees. Line a rimmed baking sheet with foil.

Drain the water chestnuts. Place the brown sugar in a bowl, dip each water chestnut in sugar to coat, wrap it in bacon, and skewer it with a toothpick. The bacon will not go all the way around the water chestnut but just enough to be secured.

Arrange the pieces on the baking sheet. About 30 minutes before serving, place them in the oven and bake until the bacon starts to crisp. Remove from the oven, arrange on a platter, and serve.

Is using fresh water chestnuts that have to be peeled worth the effort for this recipe? Probably not.

Mini Baked Crab Cakes

THREE GENERATIONS IN MY FAMILY HAVE ENJOYED THESE CRAB CAKES. THEY ARE PERFECT FOR ANY KIND OF CELEBRATION, AND THEY ARE HEALTHIER THAN THE FRIED ONES. WHEN I GOT MARRIED THESE WERE AMONG THE FIRST DISHES I MADE, AND THEY WERE A BIG HIT.

MAKES ABOUT 36

1 POUND LUMP CRABMEAT

2 LARGE EGGS

¼ CUP FINELY MINCED SCALLIONS

¼ CUP MINCED PARSLEY

1 CLOVE GARLIC, MINCED

2 TEASPOONS DIJON MUSTARD

1 TABLESPOON DRY MUSTARD

2 TEASPOONS WORCESTERSHIRE SAUCE

1¼ CUPS FINE DRY BREAD CRUMBS

¾ CUP MAYONNAISE

SALT

CAYENNE TO TASTE

2 TABLESPOONS EXTRA VIRGIN OLIVE OIL

1 TEASPOON PAPRIKA

A FEW DROPS OF TABASCO SAUCE

Place the crabmeat in a large bowl with the eggs and mix to combine. Add the scallions, parsley, garlic, mustards, and Worcestershire sauce. Blend together with a fork. Add ¼ cup of the bread crumbs, fold in 2 tablespoons of the mayonnaise, and season with salt and cayenne.

Form the mixture into tiny patties, using a scant tablespoon of the mixture for each. Put them on a plate, cover with plastic, and refrigerate until cool (the cakes are easier to handle when chilled).

Heat the oil in a medium skillet over medium heat, add the remaining bread crumbs, and stir until well blended. Transfer the bread crumbs to a shallow bowl. Remove the crab cakes from the refrigerator. Cover a baking sheet with foil. Gently dip the crab cakes into the bread crumbs and arrange them on the baking sheet. Refrigerate until 30 minutes before serving.

Preheat the oven to 375 degrees. Place the crab cakes in the oven and bake until lightly browned, about 25 minutes. Meanwhile, mix the remaining mayonnaise with the paprika and Tabasco to taste. When the crab cakes are done, use the back end of a spoon to park a small dab of the seasoned mayonnaise on top of each, and serve.

❧ The crab cakes can be slightly underbaked and reheated to crisp and ❧ brown them just before serving. Instead of dabbing the sauce on each, a little dish of sauce for dipping can go on the tray for passing the crab cakes.

Double Salmon Mousse

ISABELLE, THE WOMAN WHO COOKED FOR MY PARENTS-IN-LAW, WAS ONCE GIVEN THE TASK OF TEACHING ME HOW TO COOK ONE SUMMER WITH LESSONS TWO DAYS A WEEK. IT WAS IMPOSSIBLE. SO SHE WOULD COOK A DINNER, WHICH MY FRIENDS ALL ADORED, AND MY HUSBAND PETER AND I WERE VERY POPULAR THAT YEAR. THIS INCREDIBLY ELEGANT DISH IS THE ONE RECIPE THAT HAS ENDURED IN MY REPERTOIRE. IT NEVER FAILS TO ELICIT RAVES.

MAKES 12 OR MORE SERVINGS

1 CUP DRY WHITE WINE

1 POUND SALMON STEAK, PREFERABLY WILD PACIFIC KING OR SOCKEYE

SALT AND FRESHLY GROUND WHITE PEPPER

1 ENVELOPE PLAIN GELATIN

2 TABLESPOONS LEMON JUICE

½ CUP CHOPPED SWEET ONION

½ CUP MAYONNAISE

½ TEASPOON PAPRIKA

½ CUP HEAVY CREAM

½ CUP PLAIN YOGURT

¼ POUND SMOKED SALMON, CHOPPED

1 TABLESPOON FINELY MINCED CHIVES

1 ENGLISH CUCUMBER, SLICED PAPER THIN

THIN-SLICED PUMPERNICKEL TRIANGLES FOR SERVING

Place the wine in a saucepan, add 1 cup water, and bring to a slow simmer. Add the salmon and poach for 8 minutes. Allow to cool in the broth for 20 minutes. Remove the salmon, discard the skin and bones, and pat it dry on paper towels. Break it into chunks. Reheat the poaching broth. Season to taste with salt and pepper.

Place the gelatin, lemon juice, and onion in a blender. Strain the hot poaching broth, add ½ cup of it to the blender, and blend on high speed for

40 seconds. (Reserve the remaining strained broth to use as fish stock; it can be frozen.) Add the mayonnaise, paprika, and poached salmon and blend on high speed. Add the cream and blend again. Add the yogurt, blend, then transfer the contents of the blender to a bowl. Fold in the smoked salmon and chives.

Pack the mixture into a 4-cup mold, either round or an oblong terrine. Cover and refrigerate for at least 4 hours, until firm.

To unmold the mousse, run a knife around the edge of the mold, then dip the bottom of the mold briefly into hot water. Hold a serving plate over the mold, then invert the two together. Decorate it with cucumber slices and serve with pumpernickel triangles for spreading.

❧ Years ago, canned salmon was the ingredient of choice because good ❧
fresh salmon was not as available in fish markets as it is now.
Try to use wild Pacific salmon—it is better for the environment than
farmed salmon. Replacing the fresh and smoked salmon in this recipe
with poached fresh trout and smoked trout is a nice variation.

Susan's Pork and Clementine Bites

My friend Susan Binger would make these pork bites to serve at black tie chamber concerts in the wood-paneled parlor of her Upper East Side brownstone. Her recipe evolved over the years, gradually becoming spicier. I have added my own touches.

1 CUP FRESH ORANGE JUICE

JUICE OF 2 LIMES

¼ CUP SOY SAUCE

1½ TEASPOONS CHINESE FIVE-SPICE POWDER

2 POUNDS WELL-TRIMMED BONELESS PORK SHOULDER,
CUT INTO ¾-INCH PIECES

SALT AND FRESHLY GROUND BLACK PEPPER

6 FRESH CLEMENTINES, PEELED, DIVIDED INTO SEGMENTS, PITH REMOVED

1 TABLESPOON MINCED CILANTRO LEAVES

1 WHOLE CLEMENTINE FOR SERVING

Whisk together the orange juice, lime juice, soy sauce, and five-spice powder in a bowl. Place the pork in a heavy-duty zip-top bag, add the juice mixture, seal, place in a bowl (insurance against leaks), and refrigerate for 3 hours.

Preheat the oven to 300 degrees. Spread the pork over a baking dish large enough to hold it comfortably in a single layer. Pour on half the marinade. Season with salt and pepper. Bake uncovered for 45 minutes, basting from time to time. Increase the oven temperature to 400 degrees. Baste with the remaining marinade and bake for another 45 minutes, until the marinade has cooked down and the pork is starting to brown. Remove from the oven. If not serving immediately, cover the baking dish with foil and keep in a turned-off oven to stay warm.

Place a clementine segment on each piece of pork and secure with a toothpick or a 4-inch bamboo skewer. Sprinkle skewers with cilantro. Serve directly from the baking dish or arrange on a platter. Place a whole clementine on the platter as a pin cushion for used picks, and serve warm.

These skewered pork and orange pieces can also garnish a salad, a steaming bowl of black bean soup, or even a paella.

Roaring Twenties Coffee Bavarian Cream

THIS WAS A DESSERT THAT MY FATHER'S GREAT-AUNT USED TO SERVE
ON SPECIAL OCCASIONS IN NEW YORK BACK IN THE 1920S.

Makes 12 or more servings

2 packets plain gelatin

1 cup whole milk

1 cup brewed espresso

1 cup sugar

2 large egg whites

1 teaspoon salt

2 cups heavy cream

Small chocolate truffles for decoration, chilled

Place the gelatin in a 4-cup glass measuring cup and stir in the milk. Bring the espresso to a boil and whisk it into the milk mixture. Stir in the sugar. Transfer the mixture to a metal bowl and place it in a large bowl filled with ice and water. Stir from time to time as the mixture cools. When the mixture starts to thicken, transfer it to the bowl of an electric mixer.

Beat the mixture at high speed until it is smooth and fairly thick and lightens in color.

In a separate bowl, beat the egg whites with the salt until they hold peaks but are not dry. Fold the egg whites into the gelatin mixture.

Whip the cream until stiff and fold it into the gelatin mixture. Transfer the mixture to an 8-cup metal ring mold or another fancy mold. Cover and refrigerate for at least 6 hours.

To serve, unmold the mousse and decorate it with chocolate truffles, if you like, which can also be piled in the center of the unmolded dessert.

❧ Instead of serving the Bavarian cream as an umolded dessert, you can chill ❧
the mixture in espresso cups and serve a tray of them with demitasse spoons, each
topped with a chocolate truffle. You will be able to make 32 to 40 portions.

The Best Biscotti

THIS IS MY FAVORITE COOKIE. THE RECIPE ORIGINATED FROM A COOKING CLASS I TOOK WHILE LIVING IN FLORENCE, ITALY, DURING MY JUNIOR YEAR ABROAD IN COLLEGE. I LIKE THESE BISCOTTI BECAUSE THEY ARE CRUNCHY AND SWEET, NOT RICH AND BUTTERY LIKE MOST OTHERS I HAVE TRIED. I LOVE THIS RECIPE EVEN MORE NOW BECAUSE THEY ARE DAIRY-FREE AND MY SON, WHO IS ALLERGIC TO MILK, REALLY ENJOYS THEM. I OFTEN SERVE THESE BISCOTTI AT DINNER PARTIES, AFTER DESSERT, ONCE WE HAVE GOTTEN UP FROM THE TABLE, OR PASS THEM WITH SWEET WINE, COGNAC, AND DARK CHOCOLATES INSTEAD OF COFFEE. IT IS A FUN AND A SWEET WAY TO END AN EVENING.

MAKES ABOUT 60 COOKIES

2¼ CUPS ALL-PURPOSE FLOUR, PLUS MORE FOR DUSTING IF NEEDED

1 TEASPOON BAKING POWDER

½ TEASPOON SALT

4 LARGE EGGS

1¼ CUPS SUGAR

8 OUNCES ALMONDS, LIGHTLY TOASTED

1 LARGE EGG YOLK

Preheat the oven to 350 degrees and line a large baking sheet with parchment paper.

In a large bowl, sift the flour with the baking powder and salt. In an electric mixer, beat the eggs until foamy, gradually beating in the sugar until the mixture is very pale and thick. Stir in the flour mixture and remove the dough from the bowl to a work surface. It should be fairly soft but not sticky. A little more flour will help if it is too sticky.

Knead the dough briefly until it is smooth and flatten it into a square. Place the almonds on top, fold the dough over the almonds, and knead it to distribute the almonds. Divide it in two and roll each portion into a thick rope about 15 inches long. Place on the baking sheet. Lightly beat the egg yolk and brush it on top of each rope.

Bake until firm, about 30 minutes. Remove from the oven (keep the oven on) and set aside to cool for 20 minutes. Cut each portion into ½-inch slices on an angle. Arrange the slices on the baking sheet, standing up and close to each other but not touching. Return them to the oven and bake for 15 minutes until golden. Remove from the oven and cool.

❧ Biscotti, like the French biscuit and, for that matter, the German zweibach, ❧ means "twice-cooked," which is exactly how these cookies are made. This recipe is about as basic as can be and is open to variations. Different nuts, flavorings like anise seeds or fennel seeds, dried currants or finely chopped dates, grated citrus peel, and even ground pepper are additions to consider.

A Winter Feast
HOLIDAY DINNER

In homes across America, the most extended holiday time begins with Thanksgiving and continues all the way through New Year's, cutting a generous swath across cultures. Christmas for every Christian denomination, the Jewish eight-day Hanukkah observance, Kwanzaa for African-Americans, and, more recently the Muslim Eid are all even commemorated on United States postage stamps.

In New York, the season traditionally kicks off during the first week of December with the lighting of the Rockefeller Center Christmas tree—always a magnificent evergreen that stands as a symbol of hope. The city is already decked out in twinkling lights and the magic of the holidays is reflected in the fanciful store windows and on the faces of the children who flock to watch the Nutcracker at Lincoln Center and the Holiday Show at Radio City Music Hall. Chestnuts are roasted on street corners, and shoppers bustle along Fifth Avenue.

All the holiday celebrations—religious and secular, and often both—fill the calendar. Most of these occasions call for feasting and exchanging gifts. Gatherings with family, sharing, and most of all, an outpouring of caring for others mark the holidays.

"For Christmas, my sister had the idea to start a cookbook so we could preserve all the family favorites. Each year we add a few more and remember others that we want to track down. Everyone contributes and the new recipes are distributed during Christmas. There's nothing like food to bring back the family memories!"

—Barbara McLaughlin

"With lots of stops to make on Christmas day, my parents started a family tradition of a formal Christmas Eve dinner featuring beef tenderloin. We would then go to midnight Mass. One year to our astonishment, Santa had visited while we sat patiently at church."

—Chesie Breen

"We always have a party on Christmas Eve with close family and friends. We open up our whole apartment and there are children everywhere! We always serve kir royale (an aperitif made with Champagne and a little bit of crème de cassis, currant liqueur) in keeping with the red Christmas theme and the festive mood."

— Elizabeth Fuller

"My husband's family always makes pancakes from scratch on Christmas morning, a tradition he carries on with our daughters after their visit from Santa."

—Kathy Thomas

⌐ THE MENU ⌐

SMOOTH BROCCOLI SOUP

ROASTED POTATO CAKES

OSSO BUCO IN BIANCO

POACHED CRANBERRIES AND QUINCE

SPANISH CHRISTMAS COOKIES

HUNGARIAN WALNUT KIFLI

SNOWY DIVINITY CANDY

This holiday menu covers many observances and is a compilation of some of the more festive dishes contributed for this book. The broccoli soup is a tradition in one home, the potato cakes in another, and the Christmas sweets have various origins; but all have been passed down from one generation to another. The dishes are also suited to advance preparation.

A rich white wine, a Burgundy or a California chardonnay, would be a perfect complement to this menu.

ALSO SUGGESTED: *Ebba's Swedish Apple Cider Punch (page 175), Butternut Squash Soup with Parmesan and Sage (page 160), Short Ribs Bourguignon (page 38), Cornbread–Pecan Stuffing with Dried Fruit (page 180), Sweet and Sour Red Cabbage (page 167), Green Beans That Cooked "All Night" (page 183), Fried Green Apples (page 81), Ellie's Double Coconut Layer Cake (page 56)*

Smooth Broccoli Soup

MY MOTHER MAKES THIS SOUP EVERY THANKSGIVING—BY NOVEMBER
EVERYONE CRAVES IT. IT SUITS OTHER HOLIDAY DINNERS, TOO.

Makes 8 servings

1 LARGE BUNCH BROCCOLI, CHOPPED

1 HEAD GARLIC, SEPARATED INTO CLOVES AND WRAPPED IN CHEESECLOTH

3 STALKS CELERY, COARSELY CHOPPED

6 CUPS CHICKEN STOCK

6 SPRIGS PARSLEY

1 CUP HEAVY CREAM

Salt and freshly ground black pepper

In a large saucepan, combine the broccoli, garlic, celery, stock, and parsley. Bring to a boil over medium-high heat, cover, reduce the heat, and simmer for 30 minutes.

Remove the bag of garlic, run under cold water, then press the soft pulp from each clove back into the soup. Discard the peels.

Puree the contents of the saucepan in a blender in small batches, never filling the blender jar more than halfway. Pour the puree into a large bowl. Clean the pot, return the puree to it, and bring it to a simmer. Add the cream, season with salt and pepper to taste, and return to a simmer. Remove from the heat, set aside until ready to serve, then reheat just before serving.

You can use the broccoli stems as well as the florets in this recipe.
You might also try making it with cauliflower instead of broccoli.

"We dig into the leftovers in the kitchen on Christmas night. There are people of all ages. It's a nice way to finish off Christmas and to avoid letdown."
— Nicole Limbocker

Roasted Potato Cakes

My mother-in-law serves these potato cakes as a side dish with roast beef or sliced steak. The preparation, involving baking the potatoes instead of frying them, is easy, and the basic potato mixture can be varied, by adding mushrooms for example. Sometimes I serve the cakes as a luncheon dish, topped with smoked salmon and whipped cream cheese or crème fraîche and a green salad alongside.

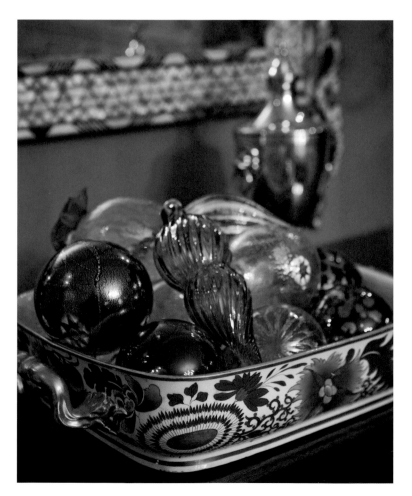

3 LARGE BAKING POTATOES, SCRUBBED
SALT
6 TABLESPOONS (¾ STICK) UNSALTED BUTTER, MELTED
¼ CUP HEAVY CREAM OR PLAIN WHOLE MILK YOGURT
1 LARGE EGG YOLK, BEATEN
FRESHLY GROUND BLACK PEPPER
1 MEDIUM ONION, CHOPPED

Place the potatoes in a saucepan and add salted water to cover. Bring to a boil and cook until tender, about 30 minutes. Drain and cool, then peel and pass them through a ricer into a large bowl. Add 3 tablespoons of the butter and the cream or yogurt. Mix in the egg yolk. Season to taste with salt and pepper. Cover and refrigerate; the cakes will be easier to form if the mixture is cold.

Preheat the oven to 375 degrees. Line a baking sheet with foil and lightly butter the foil.

Heat 1 tablespoon of the remaining butter in a small skillet over medium heat, add the onion, and sauté until golden, about 5 minutes.

Form the potato mixture into 8 patties. Use the back of a spoon to make a depression in the center of each and place some of the onion in it. Lightly flatten the cakes with a spatula and transfer them to the baking sheet. Bake for about 40 minutes, until lightly browned. Brush with the remaining 2 tablespoons butter and serve.

❋ These potato cakes are easily made in advance and reheated, or even frozen. ❋
Make them very small, no more than 2 inches in diameter, and you have a nice hors
d'oeuvre—serve with a dab of sour cream and a few grains of caviar on top.

"The first night of Hanukkah is the most significant, when we light the first candles in the silver menorah that I got as a wedding present. Then I am in the kitchen frying latkes (potato pancakes) made with grated potato, onions, eggs, and flour or matzoh meal. I fry them in oil — it has to be oil because it's a symbol of the holiday commemorating a 'miracle' when the lamp burned in the temple for eight nights though there was only enough oil for one."

— Florence Fabricant

"When we gather at my father-in-law's home for Christmas dinner, there is one very special tradition I have come to love. When we sit down we all hold hands and sing the first verse of 'Silent Night.' At this moment, any stresses leading up to this special day are replaced with the serene and tranquil thoughts of the meaning of Christmas."
— Catherine Carey

Osso Buco in Bianco

I have no idea where this recipe came from—all I know is that
I seldom share it because it is so delicious!

Makes 8 servings

8 slices osso buco (veal shanks), about 1 inch thick
(about 3 pounds)
¼ cup all-purpose flour
Salt and freshly ground black pepper
½ cup extra virgin olive oil
3 tablespoons unsalted butter
About 2 cups dry white wine
2 tablespoons grated lemon zest
5 tablespoons finely chopped flat-leaf parsley
1 clove garlic, minced

Pat dry the veal with paper towels. Season the flour with salt and pepper and place it on a plate. Dredge the veal on both sides with the seasoned flour.

Heat the oil and butter in a 6-quart sauté pan with a cover over medium-high heat. Brown the veal, a few pieces at a time, without crowding, on both sides, then remove the slices to a platter. Whisk in 1½ cups of the wine. Return the meat to the pan, baste it, cover the pan, reduce the heat, and cook at a gentle simmer for about 2 hours, until the veal is very tender, adding more wine as needed.

Transfer the shanks to a warm platter.

Add the lemon zest, parsley, and garlic to the pan and stir, scraping the bottom. Season the sauce with more salt and pepper if needed. Return the shanks to the pan, along with any juices from the platter. Baste again. Set aside until serving time, reheat briefly, then arrange on a platter and serve.

The mixture of lemon zest, parsley, and garlic, called gremolata in Italy, is a traditional condiment to serve alongside a classic osso buco. This is not a classic osso buco, though, as there is no dicing of carrot, celery, and onion to start and no tomato in the braising liquid, but stirring the gremolata into this simple white wine sauce adds terrific fresh flavor panache.

Poached Cranberries and Quince

TART QUINCES HAVE FASCINATED ME EVER SINCE I READ *The Owl and the Pussycat* AS A CHILD. "THEY DINED ON MINCE AND SLICES OF QUINCE . . ." QUINCES, AN AUTUMN AND EARLY WINTER FRUIT, LOOK LIKE YELLOW-GREEN APPLES, BUT WHEN RAW, THEY HAVE A HARD, DRY TEXTURE AND A SOUR FLAVOR. COOKING TRANSFORMS THEM, GIVING THEM A LUSH TEXTURE, A GENTLE TART-SWEETNESS, AND A LOVELY ROSE COLOR, WHICH IS ENHANCED BY THE ADDITION OF THE CRANBERRIES.

Makes 8 servings

3 CUPS SUGAR

1½ CUPS DRIED CRANBERRIES

6 FRESH QUINCES

6 TABLESPOONS FRESH POMEGRANATE SEEDS, OPTIONAL

UNSWEETENED WHIPPED CREAM FOR SERVING, OPTIONAL

Place the sugar in a 3-quart saucepan and stir in 6 cups water and the cranberries. Bring to a simmer over medium heat and simmer, stirring, until the sugar dissolves. Remove from the heat.

Peel and core the quinces and cut them into eighths, doing this one quince at a time and placing the cut slices in the sugar syrup as they are cut. Use a very sharp paring knife, as the flesh of raw quince is hard.

Once the quinces have been prepared, bring them to a slow simmer. Place a round of parchment paper in the pot on top of the quinces to keep them submerged. Simmer gently until the quinces are tender, 1 hour or longer. Allow the quinces to cool in the syrup, then refrigerate for at least several hours, preferably overnight.

To serve, spoon the quinces and cranberries into glass dishes or goblets and scatter pomegranate seeds on top, if using. Drop a cloud of whipped cream on each serving if you like.

This compote can be served from a large bowl. And it is not just for dessert—the fruit is a delicious accompaniment to roast duck and seared duck breasts.

ALICIA BOUZÁN-CORDON

Spanish Christmas Cookies

In Spanish these are called Mantecados, and they are traditionally served with Anis del Mono, a typical Spanish liqueur that is similar to Italian sambuca. The recipe comes from my mother, Laura Bouzán.

MAKES ABOUT 4 DOZEN

3 cups all-purpose flour, plus more for rolling

1 teaspoon salt

2½ tablespoons granulated sugar

12 tablespoons (1½ sticks) unsalted butter

Juice of ½ lemon

Sifted confectioners' sugar for dredging

Ground cinnamon for decoration

Preheat the oven to 350 degrees and line 2 baking sheets with parchment paper.

Place the flour, salt, and granulated sugar in a food processor and pulse to combine. Pulse in the butter and lemon juice to make a smooth dough. Transfer the dough to a lightly floured work surface and let it rest for about 20 minutes.

Roll the dough to a ¾-inch thickness. Use a 2½-inch round cutter to make small cookies. Use the end of a wooden spoon to make a deep depression in the center of each and place on the baking sheets.

Place in the oven and bake for about 15 minutes, until the cookies are firm but not colored. Remove from the oven and cool on a rack.

Dredge the cookies in confectioners' sugar and dust with a sprinkle of cinnamon.

Tender, sugar-dusted butter cookies are traditional for the holidays in many other countries, including Mexico, Greece, and Italy.

Hungarian Walnut Kifli

⁓

THIS RECIPE WAS USED BY MY GRANDMOTHER AND MOTHER AND HAS BEEN MADE BY MANY GENERATIONS OF HUNGARIAN WOMEN. THESE RICH PASTRIES ARE VERY ADDICTIVE AND THEY MELT IN YOUR MOUTH. THEY ARE A HOLIDAY TREAT IN HUNGARY, OFTEN MADE AT CHRISTMASTIME.

MAKES ABOUT 40

2 CUPS ALL-PURPOSE FLOUR, PLUS MORE FOR ROLLING

1 TEASPOON BAKING POWDER

¼ TEASPOON SALT

2 STICKS (½ POUND) UNSALTED BUTTER

8 OUNCES CREAM CHEESE

⅓ CUP SUGAR

1 TEASPOON GRATED LEMON ZEST

5 OUNCES FINELY CHOPPED WALNUTS (ABOUT ½ CUP)

1 LARGE EGG YOLK

Place the flour, baking powder, and salt in a food processor. Process briefly to blend. Dice the butter and cream cheese and add them to the food processor. Process with several long pulses until all the ingredients are combined, then process until a ball of dough forms. Shape it into a disk. The dough can be rolled immediately, but it's better to refrigerate it for 30 minutes before rolling.

Meanwhile, preheat the oven to 350 degrees.

Mix the sugar with 3 tablespoons water in a small saucepan. Place over medium heat and simmer until the sugar dissolves. Stir in the lemon zest and walnuts. Set aside.

Roll the dough to a ¹⁄₁₆-inch thickness on a lightly floured work surface. Trim it with a knife to make a rectangle and cut it into 3-inch squares. Place a scant teaspoon of the walnut filling on each square.

Roll the squares on the diagonal, from point to point, then curve each pastry slightly. Place them on a baking sheet. Press the scraps together and roll again to make additional pastries.

Beat the egg yolk with a teaspoon of water and brush on the pastries. Place in the oven and bake until golden, 30 to 35 minutes.

❧ These pastries take to various fillings. A half cup of Hungarian prune or ❧ apricot butter (lekvar) or any kind of jam can be used in place of the walnut paste. Poppy seed paste, which is now available from baking supply houses in cans, may also be used. With their tender cream cheese crust, these sweets are close cousins to Jewish rugelach—add more cinnamon and some raisins to the walnut filling and you practically have them. In fact, the pastry is a terrific addition to any cook's repertory to use (cut in rounds and folded over) to make savory hors d'oeuvres with a filling of mushroom duxelles, minced meat, or cheese. And they also freeze beautifully, no matter how they are filled.

"The big event is a dinner Christmas night. There is a fairly lavish menu, which I vary at my peril. A very rich and comforting chicken dish in pastry, usually insisted upon by the slimmest of my friends, is the hot dish. Sliced cold beef with horseradish sauce, ham with mustard sauce, smoked turkey with cranberry sauce, and smoked salmon with onions, lemons, and capers are all accompanied by various breads. There are also lots of Christmas cookies, often made at home but just as easily found at various shops in New York if time runs out."

— Leslie Perkin

BARBARA MCLAUGHLIN

Snowy Divinity Candy

WHEN I GOT MARRIED, MY GREAT-AUNT FLORENCE GAVE ME THIS RECIPE FOR A HOLIDAY TREAT THAT'S POPULAR IN MINNESOTA. SHE WONDERED IF I, AS A YOUNG WOMAN LIVING AND WORKING IN NEW YORK CITY, WOULD EVER HAVE TIME TO COOK. SHE TOLD ME THAT SHE THOUGHT SHE HAD MADE MORE THAN 100 BATCHES OF THIS DIVINITY— OFTEN USING IT AS GIFTS DURING THE HOLIDAY SEASON. THE CANDY ALSO SERVED AS A FINISHING TOUCH TO AN ALL-WHITE MEAL THAT MY FAMILY WOULD PREPARE TO CELEBRATE SANTA LUCIA DAY (ON DECEMBER 13).

MAKES ABOUT 50 CANDIES

1 TABLESPOON UNSALTED BUTTER, SOFTENED

2 LARGE EGG WHITES

2 CUPS SUGAR

½ CUP LIGHT CORN SYRUP

1 CUP CHOPPED WALNUTS

1 TEASPOON VANILLA EXTRACT

Use the butter to grease a large baking sheet.

Place the egg whites in an electric mixer and whisk until just starting to form peaks.

Put the sugar, light corn syrup, and ½ cup water in a saucepan. Bring to a boil over medium heat and cook until the mixture reaches 270 degrees (hard-ball stage) on a candy thermometer. Start beating the egg whites again on high speed and slowly pour in the sugar syrup as they are being whipped. Keep beating until the mixture is stiff and shiny and holds its shape on a spoon.

Quickly fold in the walnuts and vanilla. Spoon mounds of the mixture on the baking sheet, set aside to firm up, then store in an airtight container.

A standing electric mixer is essential for making this recipe.

A Sparkling Soirée
NEW YEAR'S EVE

The most famous New Year's tradition in New York is, of course, the glittering ball drop in Times Square as the last seconds are counted down. In Central Park there are also fireworks and the Midnight Run (an informal four-mile race with many runners dressed up in costumes). A performance at the philharmonic or the opera is another celebratory classic, followed by dinner and Champagne. But most New Yorkers will probably tell you that they prefer home gatherings, where the television is turned on shortly before midnight to watch the festivities of revelers around the world. Invitations to dinner parties at apartments that offer a view of the fireworks over the park are especially coveted.

✦ THE MENU ✦

SMOKED SALMON CANAPÉS

ANN'S POLENTA WITH WILD MUSHROOM RAGOÛT

FESTIVE BOUILLABAISSE

BIBB AND AVOCADO SALAD

LUCKY NEW YEAR'S CAKE

"Unlike Christmas, New Year's Eve is always small—four to eight couples— black tie, seated, and reserved for the closest of friends. Guests arrive at about 9 p.m., and Champagne, wine, or other drinks and hors d'oeuvres are offered. Then we sit down at about 10. The dinner, a once-a-year menu, usually starts with smoked salmon embellished with caviar. Dessert is usually accompanied by party crackers and other silly favors. Sometimes we have so much fun that we entirely miss the midnight madness."
— Leslie Perkin

"We invite friends to our country house for the weekend and make New Year's Eve a potluck dinner with Champagne."
—Leslie Heaney

ALSO SUGGESTED: *Annie's Eggnog (page 193), Tailgate Deviled Eggs (page 123), Toasted Cheese Puffs (page 194), Butternut Squash Soup with Parmesan and Sage (page 160), Beef Stroganoff in a New York Minute (page 164), Osso Buco in Bianco (page 220), Lemon-Fennel Risotto (page 94), Double Salmon Mousse (page 202), Roaring Twenties Coffee Bavarian Cream (page 206), Flourless Dark Chocolate Cake (page 42), The Best Biscotti (page 208)*

"Since my daughter has spent much time in Spain, we have now adopted one of the country's traditions. On New Year's Eve beginning precisely at the stroke of midnight, each guest is given twelve grapes. The challenge is to eat them all before the clock stops tolling—an accomplishment that brings good luck of course."

—Leslie Perkin

New Year's Eve dinner is served late. Smoked salmon and caviar, with Champagne or sparkling wine, are crowd-pleasing, rather traditional starters. And even though some hosts and hostesses might indulge guests with rich main courses like veal with morels in cream sauce, something lighter, like the bouillabaisse recipe included here, would be another welcome option.

Except for adding the fish and seafood to the bouillabaisse and putting the final dressing on the salad, everything on this menu can be prepared in advance, a boon for a dinner that, in New York, might follow an evening at a special concert or the theater.

Champagne can be poured throughout, starting with a dry brut for the canapés, then a rosé with the main course, and following with an off-dry sparkler with dessert and toasts. But shifting to a white wine or a light red wine, like a pinot noir, would be another option for the main course.

Smoked Salmon Canapés

I AM A SUCKER FOR THE CLASSICS, TWEAKING THEM A BIT PERHAPS, BUT NEVER GOING OUT ON A LIMB AND CHALLENGING MY GUESTS. SMOKED SALMON AND CAVIAR ARE LOVELY WITH CHAMPAGNE, BUT INSTEAD OF TOAST ROUNDS OR BREAD I LIKE TO USE CUCUMBERS.

MAKES ABOUT 24 CANAPÉS

½ ENGLISH CUCUMBER
¼ POUND SMOKED SALMON, SLICED
1 OUNCE STURGEON CAVIAR OR SALMON OR TROUT ROE

Peel the cucumber and cut it into slices less than ¼ inch thick. Place the slices on paper towels and cover with paper towels.

Cut the salmon slices in strips about ½ inch wide and 4 inches long.

Arrange the dried cucumber slices on a serving platter. Loosely roll the strips of salmon and place one in the center of each cucumber slice. Top each with a few grains of caviar or roe.

There are many, many choices when it comes to smoked salmon. I prefer Scottish or Irish. As for the caviar, the same holds true. Farmed American sturgeon caviar is excellent, and it is not necessary to go beyond it, but salmon roe or Carolina trout roe would be fine substitutes.

"We're usually on holiday in the Bahamas over New Year's. We enjoy getting dressed up and going out to parties at our club there. The Junkanoo, a local festive parade, comes through at midnight. This year, for a change, we returned home on New Year's Eve and had a meal of pizza, caviar served on crispy potato chips, and Champagne. The children made their own Junkanoo Parade running through the house banging pots and pans. It was as much fun as we have ever had."

—Chesie Breen

Ann's Polenta with Wild Mushroom Ragoût

THIS RECIPE COMES FROM ANN WOLF, A WONDERFUL HOSTESS AND
DEAR FRIEND IN HOUSTON, TEXAS. THE COMBINATION OF TEXTURES
AND FLAVORS MAKE IT A STAND-OUT DISH.

MAKES 6 SERVINGS

2 OUNCES DRIED PORCINI MUSHROOMS

SALT

1 CUP YELLOW POLENTA

FRESHLY GROUND BLACK PEPPER

¼ CUP FINELY CHOPPED FLAT-LEAF PARSLEY LEAVES

¼ CUP FRESH THYME LEAVES

¾ CUP FRESHLY GRATED PARMIGIANO-REGGIANO

2 OUNCES SOFT GOAT CHEESE

1½ TABLESPOONS EXTRA VIRGIN OLIVE OIL

2 SHALLOTS, CHOPPED

1 TABLESPOON BALSAMIC VINEGAR

1 CUP CHICKEN STOCK

Preheat the oven to 350 degrees.

Bring 4 cups water to a boil in a saucepan. Remove from the heat, add
the mushrooms, and set aside to soak for 30 minutes. Drain the mushrooms
well and place them on paper towels. Reserve the liquid in the saucepan,
bring it to a simmer, and season with salt. Slowly pour the polenta into the
simmering liquid, stirring constantly. Cook over low heat for about 20
minutes, stirring often and adding more water if needed. Season with pepper.

Fold in half the parsley and thyme, half the Parmigiano-Reggiano, and
the goat cheese.

Grease a baking dish with ½ tablespoon of the oil and spread the polenta in it. Place in the oven and bake for 20 minutes.

Meanwhile, squeeze as much moisture as possible from the mushrooms and chop them. Heat the remaining 1 tablespoon oil in a skillet over medium heat, add the shallots and chopped mushrooms, and sauté until the shallots are tender, about 5 minutes. Add the vinegar and the chicken stock and cook until the mixture is slightly syrupy. Season with salt and pepper.

To serve, cut the polenta into squares and place on plates. Spoon some of the mushroom mixture on each, dust with remaining herbs, and sprinkle with the remaining Parmigiano-Reggiano.

For this recipe it's important to use a good-quality balsamic vinegar, at least ten years old.

Festive Bouillabaisse

My husband and I make this bouillabaisse together. It works for a formal dinner party or a casual buffet. We either serve it from a big ceramic bowl or from the pot in which it cooked. At a buffet our guests help themselves to portions in deep bowls, with bread and salad on the side.

Makes 6 servings

Generous pinch of saffron threads

¼ cup extra virgin olive oil, plus more for serving

1 leek, cleaned, trimmed, and chopped

2 stalks celery, chopped

1 medium onion, chopped

½ cup chopped fennel

2 cloves garlic, minced

1 bay leaf

4 sprigs fresh thyme

3 cups canned crushed tomatoes

1½ cups clam juice

About 1½ cups dry white wine

½ teaspoon fennel seeds, crushed

Salt and freshly ground black pepper

18 mussels, scrubbed

12 large shrimp, shelled and deveined

1½ pounds black sea bass, red snapper, or flounder fillets, cut into 12 pieces

Crushed red chile flakes, optional

Place the saffron in a small bowl, add ½ cup boiling water, and set aside. In a large pot, heat the oil over medium heat. Add the leek, celery, onion, fennel, and garlic. Cover and cook for about 5 minutes to wilt the vegetables. Add the bay leaf, thyme, tomatoes, clam juice, wine, and fennel seeds. Bring to a simmer and cook, covered, for about 5 minutes.

Add the saffron and its soaking liquid and simmer, uncovered, for about 15 minutes more. Remove the bay leaf.

Bring back to a steady simmer and add more wine if needed. Season to taste with the salt and pepper.

Add the mussels, cook for 5 minutes, then add the shrimp. Cook another 5 minutes, then add the fish. Reduce the heat to very low and simmer until the

mussels have opened and the shrimp and fish have cooked through. Remove any mussels that haven't opened. Check the seasoning, adding some red chile flakes if desired and an extra drizzle of oil. Serve with croutons or crusty bread.

❧ In France, bouillabaisse is a rustic dish, the seafood changing based on market availability. ☙ For example, some scrubbed littleneck clams might be included. And if your market has big blue prawns, they would be a terrific addition. Small parboiled potatoes can also be added about ten minutes before the seafood is put in. Alongside the bouillabaisse, a garlicky mayonnaise (aïoli) or a spicy one (rouille) are often served as condiments.

EUGENIE NIVEN GOODMAN

Bibb and Avocado Salad

I SERVE THIS SALAD OFTEN, AND ALWAYS WITH MY BOUILLABAISSE. IT WAS MY GRANDFATHER'S FAVORITE SALAD. WHENEVER WE WENT TO PHILADELPHIA TO VISIT HIM, THIS WAS ALWAYS THE SALAD THAT HE SERVED. HE WAS VERY PARTICULAR ABOUT HIS FOOD AND CONSIDERED BIBB LETTUCE TO BE THE BEST LETTUCE. IT BECAME MY MOTHER'S FAVORITE AND IS NOW MY FAVORITE TOO.

MAKES 6 SERVINGS

2 RIPE BUT FIRM AVOCADOS, PEELED, PITTED, AND DICED
3 TABLESPOONS LEMON JUICE
1 TABLESPOON DIJON MUSTARD
5 TABLESPOONS EXTRA VIRGIN OLIVE OIL
6 SMALL HEADS BIBB LETTUCE, CORED AND TRIMMED
¼ CUP MINCED CHIVES
SALT AND FRESHLY GROUND BLACK PEPPER

Place the avocados in a salad bowl and toss with the lemon juice. Beat the mustard and oil together and add to the bowl. Tear the lettuce into small pieces and place in the bowl. Add the chives, toss, season with salt and pepper, and serve.

In winter, when farm-fresh lettuce is scarce, small heads of Bibb lettuce are often the best option.

"We almost always spend New Year's at home with another family and our children. The children eat earlier and we set a very festive table for them with crackers, streamers, and noisemakers. The grown-ups have dinner later, and we make predictions about the Oscars, sports, celebrities, and politics. We write them down, and the next New Year's Eve the person who did best receives a bottle of Champagne!"
—Elizabeth Fuller

Lucky New Year's Cake

THIS CAKE IS TRADITIONALLY SERVED ON NEW YEAR'S DAY IN GREEK HOMES. A COIN IS HIDDEN INSIDE, AND PORTIONS ARE SLICED FOR EACH MEMBER OF THE HOUSEHOLD, STARTING WITH THE HEAD OF THE HOUSEHOLD. THE PERSON WHO FINDS THE COIN IS GUARANTEED GOOD LUCK IN THE COMING YEAR. MY FAMILY IS NOT ALWAYS TOGETHER BY THE TIME NEW YEAR'S ARRIVES, SO MY MOTHER BAKES THE CAKE AND SLICES A PIECE FOR EACH OF HER CHILDREN. THEN SHE CALLS THE LUCKY ONE OF US TO WISH US WELL. (SOMEHOW, MYSTERIOUSLY, EVERY YEAR THERE SEEMS TO BE MORE THAN ONE WINNER.)

MAKES 8 SERVINGS

6 TABLESPOONS (¾ STICK) UNSALTED BUTTER, SOFTENED
1½ CUPS ALL-PURPOSE FLOUR
3 LARGE EGGS
¾ CUP SUGAR
JUICE AND GRATED ZEST OF 1 ORANGE
1 OUNCE BRANDY OR GRAND MARNIER
1 TEASPOON BAKING POWDER
WHOLE BLANCHED ALMONDS FOR DECORATION

Preheat the oven to 350 degrees. Use a little of the butter to grease a 9-inch round cake pan. Dust with some of the flour.

Separate 2 of the eggs. Use an electric mixer to beat the egg whites until fairly stiff. Transfer them to another bowl. Place the egg yolks in the bowl of the mixer, beat briefly, then beat in ⅔ cup of the sugar until thick and light. Add the butter and beat another 2 to 3 minutes. Beat in the orange zest. Mix the orange juice and brandy together and stir into the batter. By hand add a little of the flour and fold in a spoonful of the beaten egg whites.

Mix the baking powder with the remaining flour and fold it in, then fold in the rest of the egg whites. Spread the batter into the pan. Wrap a coin in foil and tuck it into the cake. Beat the remaining egg with the remaining sugar and spread on top of the cake. Decorate the cake with almonds to spell out the numerals of the New Year.

Place in the oven and bake for about 45 minutes, until a cake tester comes out clean. Cool on a rack and remove from the pan.

❧ In some countries a dried bean is used as a good luck charm instead of ❧ a coin. In France they sell little porcelain beans to use. A cake like this is also served for Epiphany, the Feast of the Three Kings, on January 6.

Guide to Sources for Entertaining

Experienced party-givers know that having an inventory of sources for everything—from the smartest invitations and stunning flowers to the most delectable chocolates and petits fours—makes effortless entertaining possible. Some of the favorite venues for the contributors to this book are small, local markets in the city and the country, but there are many others, in this online age, that offer nationwide internet shopping. A few of the neighborhood shops in New York are included in the following directory, for the benefit of those who live in or near the city, but most of the sources are available on the Web.

GOURMET MARKETS:
These are markets that sell just about every category of food, for high-quality one-stop shopping, in person, by phone, or online.

AGATA & VALENTINA
1505 First Avenue
New York, NY
212-452-0690
www.agatavalentina.com

CITARELLA
www.citarella.com

DEAN & DELUCA
www.deananddeluca.com

ELI'S MANHATTAN
1411 Third Avenue
New York, NY
212-717-8100 or 866-354-3547
www.elizabar.com

FAIRWAY MARKET
2127 Broadway
New York, NY
212-595-1888
www.fairwaymarket.com

ZABAR'S
2245 Broadway
New York, NY
212- 787-2000
www.zabars.com

ZINGERMAN'S
888-636-8162
www.zingermans.com

SPECIALTY SOURCES:
In addition to the major markets,
there are many specialty sources in
New York and elsewhere.

BREAD
AMY'S BREAD
Chelsea Market
75 Ninth Avenue
New York, NY
212-462-4338
www.amysbread.com

BALTHAZAR BAKERY
80 Spring Street
New York, NY
212-965-1785
www.balthazarbakery.com

GRANDAISY BAKERY
250 West Broadway
New York, NY
212-334-9435
www.grandaisybakery.com

CHEESE
ARTISANAL CHEESE
877-797-1200
www.artisanalcheese.com

FORMAGGIO ESSEX
120 Essex Street
New York, NY
212-982-8200
www.formaggioessex.com

IDEAL CHEESE SHOP
942 First Avenue
New York, NY
800-382-0109
www.idealcheese.com

MURRAY'S CHEESE
254 Bleecker Street
New York, NY
212-243-3289 or 888-692-4339
www.murrayscheese.com

DESSERTS, CANDY, AND
CONFECTIONS
BABY CAKES
248 Broome Street
New York, NY
212-677-5047
www.babycakesnyc.com

CREATIVE CAKES
400 East 74th Street
New York, NY
212-794-9811
www.creativecakesny.com

ELENI'S COOKIES
Chelsea Market
75 Ninth Avenue
New York, NY
888-435-3647
www.elenis.com

HOPE, FAITH & GLUTTONY
718-706-6616
www.hopefaithandgluttony.com

FRAN'S CHOCOLATES
800-422-3726
www.franschocolates.com

GRAETER'S ICE CREAM
800-727-7425
www.graeters.com

IL LABORATORIO DEL GELATO
95 Orchard Street
New York, NY
212-343-9922
www.laboratoriodelgelato.com

JENI'S ICE CREAMS
614-488-3224
www.jenisicecreams.com

JACQUES TORRES CHOCOLATE
212-414-2462
www.mrchocolate.com

L.A. BURDICK HANDMADE
CHOCOLATES
800-229-2419
www.burdickchocolate.com

LA MAISON DU CHOCOLAT
1018 Madison Avenue
New York, NY
212-744-7117
www.lamaisonduchocolat.com

PAYARD PATISSERIE
1032 Lexington Avenue
New York, NY
212-717-5252
www.payard.com

SANT AMBROEUS
1000 Madison Avenue
New York, NY
212-570-2211
www.santambroeus.com

TATE'S BAKE SHOP
43 North Sea Road
Southampton, NY
631-780-6511
www.tatesbakeshop.com

ETHNIC MARKETS
DIPALO'S FINE FOODS
200 Grand Street
New York, NY
877-253-1779
www.dipaloselects.com

INGEBRETSEN'S SCANDINAVIAN
GIFTS AND FOODS
800-279-9333
www.ingebretsens.com

KALUSTYAN'S
123 Lexington Avenue
New York, NY
212-685-3451 or 800-352-3451
www.kalustyans.com

LA TIENDA
800-170-4304
www.tienda.com

MYERS OF KESWICK
634 Hudson Street
New York, NY
212-691-4194
www.myersofkeswick.com

MEATS
ALLEN BROTHERS
800-957-0111
www.allenbrothers.com

D'ARTAGNAN
800-327-8246
www.dartagnan.com

DE BRAGGA & SPITLER
www.debragga.com

GREYLEDGE FARM
Bridgewater, CT
860-350-3203
www.greyledgefarm.com

LA QUERCIA
515-981-1625
www.laquercia.us

LOBEL'S
1096 Madison Avenue
New York, NY
212-737-1372
www.lobels.com

SMITHFIELD FARMS
800-222-2110
www.smithfieldfarms.com

PREPARED FOODS
BUTTERFIELD MARKET
1114 Lexington Avenue
New York, NY
212-288-7800
www.butterfieldmarket.com

THE CLEAVER CO.
Chelsea Market
75 Ninth Avenue
New York, NY
212-741-9174
www.cleaverco.com

WILLIAM POLL
1051 Lexington Ave.
New York, NY
212-288-0501
www.williampoll.com

SEAFOOD
FISH EX
888-926-3474
www.fishex.com

HANCOCK LOBSTER
800-552-0142
www.hancockgourmetlobster.com

THE LOBSTER PLACE
Chelsea Market
75 Ninth Avenue
New York, NY
212-255-5672
www.lobsterplace.com

THE SEAFOOD SHOP
356 Montauk Highway
Wainscott, NY
631-537-0633
www.theseafoodshop.com

SMOKED FISH AND CAVIAR
BROWNE TRADING COMPANY
800-944-7848
www.brownetrading.com

PETROSSIAN
911 Seventh Avenue
New York, NY
212-245-2217
www.petrossian.com

RUSS AND DAUGHTERS
179 East Houston Street
New York, NY
212-475-4880 or 800-787-7229
www.russanddaughters.com

SEASONAL PRODUCE
GREEN THUMB ORGANIC FARM
829 Montauk Highway
Water Mill, NY
631-726-1900

ROUND SWAMP FARM
184 Three Mile Harbor Road
East Hampton, NY
631-324-4438
www.roundswampfarm.com

UNION SQUARE GREENMARKET
Union Square Park
17th Street at Broadway
New York, NY
www.cenyc.org/greenmarket

WINES AND SPIRITS

ACKER MERRALL & CONDIT
160 West 72nd Street
New York, NY
212-787-1700
www.ackerwines.com

ASTOR WINE & SPIRITS
399 Lafayette Street
New York, NY
212-674-7500
www.astorwines.com

GARNET WINES & LIQUORS
929 Lexington Avenue
New York, NY
212-772-3211
www.garnetwine.com

K & D WINES AND SPIRITS
1366 Madison Avenue
New York NY
212-289-1818
www.kdwine.com

MORRELL WINE SHOP
1 Rockefeller Plaza at 49th Street
New York, NY
212-981-1106 or 800-969-4637
www.morellwine.com

PARK AVENUE LIQUOR SHOP
292 Madison Ave
New York, NY
212-685-2442
www.parkaveliquor.com

SHERRY-LEHMANN
505 Park Avenue
New York, NY
212-838-7500
www.sherry-lehmann.com

WINES BY MORRELL
74 Montauk Highway
East Hampton, NY
631-324-1230

WINECARE STORAGE
224 12th Avenue, Suite 231
New York, NY
212-594-9590
www.winecare.com

ZACHYS WINE AND LIQUOR
16 East Parkway
Scarsdale, NY
800-723-0241
www.zachys.com

NON-FOOD SOURCES:

COOKWARE
KORIN JAPANESE TRADING CORP.
57 Warren Street
New York, NY
800-626-2172
www.korin.com

METROKITCHEN.COM
888-892-9911
www.metrokitchen.com

NEW YORK CAKE AND BAKING
SUPPLY
800-942-2539
www.nycake.com

SUR LA TABLE
www.surlatable.com

WILLIAMS-SONOMA
www.williams-sonoma.com

FLORAL DESIGN
BELLE FLEUR
134 Fifth Avenue
New York, NY
212-254-8703
www.bellefleurny.com

BLOOM
541 Lexington Avenue
New York, NY
212-832-8094
www.bloomflowers.com

HARTLEY DU PONT
Morristown, NJ
917-699-9697
www.hartleydupont.com

LENOX HILL FLORIST
1140 Lexington Ave
New York, NY
212-861-2787
www.lenoxhillflorist.com

PLAZA FLOWERS
944 Lexington Avenue
New York, NY
212-472-7565
www.plazaflowersnyc.com

RENNY & REED
505 Park Avenue
New York, NY
212-288-7000
www.rennyandreed.com

TOPIARE
51 Jobs Lane
Southampton, NY
631-287-3800

ZeZé
938 First Avenue
New York, NY
212-753-7767
www.zezeflowers.com

INVITATIONS & STATIONERY
Blacker & Kooby
1204 Madison Avenue
New York, NY
212-369-8308

Caspari
www.casparionline.com

Dempsey & Carroll
1049 Lexington Avenue
New York, NY
212-570-4800 or 877-750-1878
www.dempseyandcarroll.com

iomoi
925-282-1098
www.iomoi.com

Merrimade
800-344-4256
www.merrimade.com

Pickett's Press
917-716-7611
www.pickettspress.com

Polka Dot Pear Designs
800-675-3909
www.polkadotpear.com

Preppy Cards
212-288-4409
www.preppycards.com

The Printery
43 West Main Street
Oyster Bay, NY
516-922-3250
www.iprintery.com

LINENS, GIFTS & TABLEWARE
ABC Carpet & Home
888 & 881 Broadway
New York, NY
212-473-3000
www.abchome.com

Bloomingdale's
1000 Third Avenue
New York, NY
800-555-SHOP
www.bloomingdales.com

Bergdorf Goodman
754 Fifth Avenue
New York, NY
800-558-1855
www.bergdorfgoodman.com

CHARLOTTE MOSS
212-308-7088, extension 11
www.charlottemoss.com

CHELSEA MARKET BASKETS
Chelsea Market
75 Ninth Avenue
New York, NY
888-727-7887
www.chelseamarketbaskets.com

THE ELEGANT SETTING
31 Main Street
Southampton, NY
631-283-4747 or 888-277-8837
www.theelegantsetting.com

GRACIOUS HOME
www.gracioushome.com

JOHN ROBSHAW TEXTILES
245 West 29th Street, Suite 1501
New York, NY
212-594-6006
www.JohnRobshaw.com

J. ROAMAN
631-329-0662
www.jroaman.com

LEONTINE LINENS
3806 Magazine Street
New Orleans, LA 70115
800-876-4799
www.leontinelinens.com

LÉRON
804 Madison Avenue
New York, NY
800-954-6369
www.leron.com

LETA AUSTIN FOSTER
424 East 52nd Street
New York, NY
212-421-5918
www.letaaustinfoster.com

LEXINGTON GARDENS
1011 Lexington Avenue
New York, NY
212-861-4390
www.lexingtongardensnyc.com

MRS. MONOGRAM
629 Old Post Road
Bedford, New York
888-717-GIFT (4438)
www.mrsmonogram.com

OLD TOWN CROSSING
46 Main Street
Southampton, NY
631-283-7740

PEARL RIVER
477 Broadway
New York, NY
212-431-4770
www.pearlriver.com

D. PORTHAULT
470 Park Avenue
New York, NY
212-688-1660
www.dporthault.fr

TIFFANY & CO.
www.tiffany.com

SCULLY & SCULLY
504 Park Avenue
New York, NY
800-223-3717
www.scullyandscully.com

WILLIAM WAYNE & COMPANY
850 Lexington Avenue
New York, NY
800-318-3435
www.william-wayne.com

PARTY FAVORS &
DECORATIONS
DYLAN'S CANDY BAR
1011 Third Avenue
New York, NY
646-735-0078
www.dylanscandybar.com

E.A.T. GIFTS
1064 Madison Ave
New York, NY
212-772-0022

ORIENTAL TRADING
800-875-8480
www.orientaltrading.com

ZITOMER
969 Madison Avenue
New York, NY
212-737-5561
www.zitomer.com

Acknowledgments

The Society of Memorial Sloan–Kettering Cancer Center would like to thank Rizzoli Publications, especially Charles Miers, our beacon of excellence, for believing in us from the very beginning of this wonderful journey, and Christopher Steighner for guiding us every step of the way with his insight, wisdom, and grace. We would also like to thank Jonathan Jarrett, Jennifer Pierson and her team, and Pam Sommers and Jessica Napp for their enthusiasm in making our dreams come true.

It continues to be an honor to work with Florence Fabricant, who thought of the title *Park Avenue Potluck* that has captured the imagination of readers. While her distinguished work as a journalist and author is what defines her to our readers, what we celebrate most is her love of family and cooking that is the essence of our book. Patricia Fabricant has once again interpreted our sense and sensibilities with her design, and Ben Fink has brought our recipes and entertaining style to life with his photographs. We thank them for turning all aspects of our storytelling into a meaningful book that chronicles how we live in New York and the Hamptons, and our entertaining style for special occasions that can be replicated no matter where we live.

There are many others in New York and the Hamptons who generously contributed to our book on behalf of The Society of MSKCC and the patients whom we serve. We give our heartfelt thanks to Wines by Morrell in East Hampton; The Southampton Inn; Citarella in the Hamptons and New York; the Hampton Jitney; Old Town Crossing and Tate's Bake Shop in Southampton; Scully & Scully; Léron; D. Porthault; Belle Fleur; Bergdorf Goodman; John Robshaw; Judi Roaman; Fischer & Page; Holland Acres; Butterfield Market Catering; Laurie Lambrecht; Robert Swingle; Wendy Carduner and Steven Mellina of the Doubles Club and Clara's Cookies; George Greenfield of CreativeWell, Inc.; Bob Stein, Esq. of Pryor Cashman, LLP; Roger Parker, Esq. of MSKCC; and our neighbors Richard Willett,

Mrs. Gordon C. Dewey, and Meg Caldwell. We also toast Bill Brockschmidt and Courtney Coleman of Brockschmidt & Coleman; Robert Rufino; Tracy Bross; and Robb Whittlef of Historic Design Group for their style.

And last, we give our enduring gratitude to Leslie M. Jones, the President of The Society of MSKCC (2007–2009) to whom the torch was passed by Vera Safai, the President of The Society (2005–2007) who gave life to the *Park Avenue Potluck* series. Leslie embraced our second book with the same commitment to excellence, leadership, and authenticity that she has brought to her presidency, and it is the bellwether of our book. She and her husband, Peter, have also brought so much joy to creating this book with their love of cooking and entertaining for their family and friends.

—THE SOCIETY OF MEMORIAL SLOAN-KETTERING CANCER CENTER

For this, the follow-up to the original Park Avenue Potluck, there has been a sea change. When it comes to developing a book, the members of The Society of Memorial Sloan-Kettering Cancer Center have now become serious professionals. They made my work much easier.

The cookbook committee, led by Barbara Tollis, Kathy Thomas, and Heather Leeds, with styling coordinated by Chesie Breen and Leslie Perkin, and, representing the Society, Maryanne Greenfield, the executive director; Jacqueline Blandi, the associate director; Megan Mitchell, the special projects manager; and Lauren Robinson, the assistant; did a masterful job prying recipes from the members and convincing them to share their personal insights about entertaining and to open their gracious homes in New York and elsewhere for photography.

Ben Fink's camera work and Susan Sugarman's styling gave the book elegance and warmth, enhancing the graphic design by my daughter, Patricia Fabricant.

I shared the months of recipe testing with Sylvie Bigar, whose expertise helped to fine tune everything from sangria and popovers to filet mignon and cheesecake. And I knew I could count on Richard Fabricant to taste and critique the end results. Throughout, it was the support of the entire team at Rizzoli Publications that made *Park Avenue Potluck Celebrations* worth celebrating.

—FLORENCE FABRICANT

Conversion Chart

All conversions are approximate.

LIQUID CONVERSIONS

U.S.	METRIC
1 tsp	5 ml
1 tbs	15 ml
2 tbs	30 ml
3 tbs	45 ml
¼ cup	60 ml
⅓ cup	75 ml
⅓ cup + 1 tbs	90 ml
⅓ cup + 2 tbs	100 ml
½ cup	120 ml
⅔ cup	150 ml
¾ cup	180 ml
¾ cup + 2 tbs	200 ml
1 cup	240 ml
1 cup + 2tbs	275 ml
1¼ cups	300 ml
1⅓ cups	325 ml
1½ cups	350 ml
1⅔ cups	375 ml
1¾ cups	400 ml
1¾ cups + 2 tbs	450 ml
2 cups (1 pint)	475 ml
2½ cups	600 ml
3 cups	720 ml
4 cups (1 quart)	945 ml (1,000 ml is 1 liter)

WEIGHT CONVERSIONS

U.S./U.K.	METRIC
½ oz	14 g
1 oz	28 g
1½ oz	43 g
2 oz	57 g
2½ oz	71 g
3 oz	85 g
3½ oz	100 g
4 oz	113 g
5 oz	142 g
6 oz	170 g
7 oz	200 g
8 oz	227 g
9 oz	255 g
10 oz	284 g
11 oz	312 g
12 oz	340 g
13 oz	368 g
14 oz	400 g
15 oz	425 g
1 lb	454 g

OVEN TEMPERATURES

°F	GAS MARK	°C
250	½	120
275	1	140
300	2	150
325	3	165
350	4	180
375	5	190
400	6	200
425	7	220
450	8	230
475	9	240
500	10	260
550	Broil	290

Index